Trust in the Lord
with all your
Lean not unto your o
understanding... He will
direct your path

Rev. Justine Harif

Rev. Justine Harif
Refuge Church of Christ
106 Broadway, N.Y. 11520
Freeport, N.Y.
516-868-0400

GET OVER IT!!!

A DOWN TO EARTH LOOK AT THE ISSUES OF CHRISTIAN DIVORCE AND REMARRIAGE

Rev. Justine Hanif

authorHOUSE™

1663 LIBERTY DRIVE, SUITE 200
BLOOMINGTON, INDIANA 47403
(800) 839-8640
WWW.AUTHORHOUSE.COM

First published by AuthorHouse 08/26/05

ISBN: 1-4208-7484-5 (e)
ISBN: 1-4208-7483-7 (sc)

Library of Congress Control Number: 2005907066

Printed in the United States of America
Bloomington, Indiana

This book is printed on acid-free paper.

Table Of Contents

DEDICATION

This book is dedicated to my two children, Uriah and Elizabeth. With God's love and protection we have survived and shared so much.

ACKNOWLEDGMENTS

To my ex-husband, thank you for the struggle. It is my sincere prayer that you find your place in God and have success and happiness.

To Bishop Ronald H. Carter and Pastor Phyllis E. Carter, thank you for your leadership, prayers and love. You are tremendous teachers and preachers of the Word of God. You are an excellent example of what a successful God ordained marriage should be.

To Reverend Tina Baker thank you for your encouragement and for pushing me. Thank you for being an example of blindly obeying God.

To Valerie Montgomery, my best friend, thank you for your support, for listening and for being a friend I can lean on.

To my sister Reverend Michele Taylor, thank you for paving the way and for being a sounding board.

INTRODUCTION

Praise the Lord!!! My name is Justine Jackson Hanif and I am a member of D.C.F.A. (Divorced Church Folks Anonymous). We are an increasingly large group of church folk who secretly bleed from broken marriages.

When I was eighteen years old, I made a decision without counsel or direction from either my parents or God. I chose to marry when neither my boyfriend nor I were mature enough or stable enough to understand the commitment or challenges of marriage. I accepted Jesus Christ as my Savior two years after I married. Eleven years later, I found myself divorced with two children and the victim of emotional abuse. I was hurt, embarrassed and confused, questioning why or how God could allow this to happen to me. I considered myself faithful to God. I loved Him and I loved my husband. The problems we had were not insurmountable. Because God will withhold no good thing, and He will give us the desires of our hearts, I believed He would save my marriage. Yet I found myself divorced, and life didn't make sense. I cried for myself, I cried for the pain my children were experiencing, and I cried because I was a young woman who wanted to have companionship. However, I had no hope of remarrying due to our church doctrine. Our church organization did not believe in divorce and remarriage. Today I can say that the scripture is true and correct "And we know that all things work together for good to them that love God, to them who are the called according to His purpose" (Romans 8:28). I have learned purpose from my pain.

In July of 2003, Rev. Tina Baker, a minister of my church

spoke a prophetic word into my life. There was a word inside of me that people outside of my church needed to hear. People as far as Colorado needed to read my story. I received this prophetic word because God had been dealing with me for several years regarding writing a book. He had given me the title and theme of two books but I was unable to focus enough to write them. Although I had received this prophetic word, I did not feel the desire to begin to write either of the books.

One Sunday morning as I watched a popular pastor on the television, he asked the profound question, "What happens when the good girl gets divorced?" God spoke into my spirit, "This is the message I want you to write. What happens when the man or woman of God who is trying to faithfully serve God becomes confronted with the devastation of a failed marriage?"

The church has ignored or attempted to cover up the issue of divorce and remarriage. It is the taboo subject that leaves unanswered questions and issues that we pretend don't exist. What does happen when the "good" man or woman gets divorced? What happens when the emotionally or mentally abused spouse decides after fifteen years, they have had enough? What happens when the man or woman of God is abandoned because their spouse just doesn't want a "saved" mate? What happens when a teenage couple married because they were expecting a child and four years later they realize they don't even like each other? What happens when the physically abused wife has left the emergency room for the tenth time with a broken rib and black eye and she chooses flight rather than fight? What happens when the first lady no longer wants to cover her pastor/husband's infidelity and violation of his vows? What happens when the man who has been separated for five years must divorce or loose everything he has to his wife's creditors? What happens when the marriage could not be consummated because the spouse was not fully delivered from homosexuality or lesbianism?

What happens when the spouse gets tired of being treated for sexually transmitted diseases their partner brought home? What happens when your spouse decides they married for the wrong motive? What happens when you get tired of hiding your money from your drug addicted or gambling spouse? Who understands the pain and disappointment of being told by your spouse that he or she is leaving you because you hinder the ministry? What happens to the woman whose husband divorced her because she disobeyed his direct order not to have her illness treated by the doctor? What happens when you can no longer take your spouse's lovers knocking on your door or calling your house? There are so many ignored "What happens when" scenarios. What happens when you've prayed, fasted and begged God to save your marriage but you end up divorced?

The preacher's question rang in my ear, "What happens when the good girl gets divorced?" The spirit of the Lord said, "You know the answer to this question. You have lived the answer to this question. There are hurting children of God who need someone to deal with the reality of their divorced situation; who need to address these questions. They want to know, "How do I go on? How do I face my family, friends, and church family? How do I overcome the roller coaster of emotions I experience? How do I stay saved when I feel God has failed me? AND, WHAT ABOUT REMARRIAGE?"

My brothers and my sisters, in the pages of this labor of love, I share my personal testimony and true stories of what happens when a child of God gets divorced. I share insights into the issues and emotions we face as divorced children of God. Through this book, I want to minister to you by letting you know that you are not alone. There are men and women throughout the body of Christ who have experienced and survived divorce. They have gone through the things you are experiencing but have not shared their testimony. They were taught to keep silent about their issues and pains.

The message of this book is a simple one. Although God hates divorce, He loves His children. He wants us to be healed and whole. In order to be healed, we must get over the experience of separation and divorce and move on to become the woman or man of God He has ordained us to be. We are to move from victim to victor to more than a conqueror.

To be truthful, this book only begins to address the issue of remarriage. To date, I have not been blessed to walk down the aisle for a second time. I can only share my experience of the promise from God that I would be married again. I share with you the spiritual wrestling I experienced as a result of conflicts between God's promise and church doctrine. I can share with you the tears of conflict, and the joyous tears of God's resolution process. I can only share with you how faith and trust in God, how wrapping myself in His service and will, turned my pain into power, purpose and victory.

PRAYER

Father God, in the name of Jesus Christ, I first thank you for your grace, mercy and unconditional love. I thank you for being the lover of our souls, our keeper and our deliver. Lord, bless your children who are suffering from the pains, frustrations and disappointments of separation and divorce. As they read this book, let them experience the healing Balm of Gilead. Let them experience victory and deliverance from every demonic spirit that has been dispatched to bind them in emotional bondage. Give them a sense of hope in the midst of their storm. Help them to ignore judgmental voices and attitudes. Speak to their hearts and give them a pre-showing of their "shall be". Help them to let go of the past and move on to the future that you have prepared for them. Turn pain into power, tears into joy and defeat into victory. All these things, I count already done. I give you praise, glory and honor. IN JESUS NAME, AMEN!!!!

Chapter 1

———

I APOLOGIZE

"For in many things we offend all. If any man offend not in word, the same is a perfect man, and able to bridle the whole body" (James 3:2).

We often make assumptions and determine a course of action for someone else based upon our experience and theology. We look at other people and question their actions. We determine what's right for them. We even feel so strongly that we feel obligated to tell them our opinion or give wise words of wisdom. We sometimes share with others, the errors of this person's decisions. More often than not we have caused an offense that God requires us to deal with.

The Word of God emphasizes the importance of reconciling an offense and of keeping the doors of forgiveness open. The need to reconcile is so significant that the Word of God instructs us to resolve any aught we have against our brethren even before we bring God an offering or sacrifice. Before I can offer this book up to God. Before I can express another word. Before I can share my experiences with someone else in the hope of being a blessing, I must first apologize.

I had written several pages of this book when God arrested my thoughts and my hand. He dropped the words "I apologize" into my spirit. God showed me that I needed to apologize to those I may have offended. In the context of this book, I will share many

1

experiences I had where someone offended me in word or deed as a result of my divorce. There were people who angered me or brought tears to my eyes. They cut me with their words, but didn't know it.

As I set my pen to write, God showed me myself. In the same way others have offended or hurt me, even unintentionally, I had hurt or offended someone else. There are people out there that I owe an apology to. Although my actions or thoughts were well intentioned, I still caused an offense. I still caused pain. Every time I made assumptions about someone else's life, I became the offender. Here I am looking at how people offended me, and God said you are no different. You are just as guilty. There are people whose situations I have judged and determined how they should have handled them. I did not know their full situation. Yet I set myself up as their judge and jury.

I have a friend who was in the process of divorcing his wife. We had many discussions where I debated scripture with him. I Corinthians.7 was my sermon to him. He needed to forgive his wife and allow God to restore their marriage. After all, they were both "saved." They should have been able to overcome anything. Didn't he believe the scripture that stated that he could do all things through Jesus Christ? My friend never asked me for my opinion, but I freely and righteously gave it. I did not know anything about their marital experience. I didn't know their struggles, their issues or their history. But I pushed for reconciliation. How arrogant and self-righteous I was. I gave this brother a hard time.

Years later when I found myself divorced and God dealt with me about remarriage in my own situation, I realized my error. One day I saw this brother. As we discussed the topic of remarriage, he reminded me of our past conversations on this topic. He laughingly told me that I was not preaching the same message. I hung my head. The only thing I could do, was acknowledge my error and tell him that God had opened my understanding.

There are those who may argue that the change in my attitude and stand on divorce and remarriage is the result of compromising God's word. Now that I have experienced divorce, I have conveniently twisted God's word to meet my circumstances. Although I will not take the time to argue with them, I must agree that the experience of divorce has changed my way of thinking. I have found that experience is a good teacher. It forces one to look at circumstances, attitudes and belief systems from the inside, up close and personal. Experience causes one to grow in understanding and relationship with God. After Satan tempted Job, he was able to say, "I have heard of thee with the hearing of the ear but now I seeth thee." Although Job served God and had relationship with God, he developed a better relationship and understanding of God as a result of his difficult experience.

A bishop and former bible institute instructor would often tell his class, "We used to teach… but now we understand." He explained, that we dogmatically take a stand on an issue or belief only to have a life experience teach us the error of that belief. He stated that as a pastor, he used to teach his missionaries and ministers that they should not cry when they visit the sick in the hospital. However, he found that when he visited his own sister in the hospital, he could not stop the tears from flowing. It was then that he learned sometimes one can not help showing emotion when visiting a sick loved one. This did not make a person less of a missionary or minister; it made them human. The pastor's life experience taught him that his harsh teaching and treatment of those who cried when visiting a sick loved one was incorrect. His experience opened his understanding.

In this same way, my experience with divorce opened me up to receive a clearer understanding from God. It taught me to be more compassionate and less quick to make a judgment of other people's circumstances. Therefore I once again apologize to my divorced brother in Christ and to all those I have offended or caused pain. I apologize to all my sisters and brothers in Christ who are separated or divorced who have been wrongly weighed in the balance and found wanting because of your marital status. You may never receive an apology from those who you expected to support you but ended up judging you. They may never come to an understanding of the injury they have caused. They may never change their attitude or opinion. If the fact that they have hurt, misunderstood or judged you has kept you bound, I am standing in the gap for them so that you may be set free.

"I APOLOGIZE!!!! I am sorry for the pain caused. Please

forgive us." Accept this apology as an opening door to release your anger and pain. Open your heart to forgive and begin to be healed. Like Jesus and Stephen, you need to be able to say, "Father, forgive them for they know not what they do."

PRAYER

Father God in the name of Jesus, thank you for forgiving us of our offenses. Help us to forgive those who have offended us intentionally or without knowledge. Help us to forget the past offenses that have kept us bound and prevented us from becoming the vessel you destined us to be.

Amen!!!

Chapter 2

—◆—

GET OVER IT

When I sat down to begin writing this book, I found myself stuck on the first paragraph of the first chapter. For days, I attempted to put words to paper, but they wouldn't come. Finally, I decided to begin writing this book by starting in the middle chapters. This time, when I sat down to write, the words began to freely flow. The question I asked myself was," If God, told me to write this book, why did I have writer's block? The answer came one Sunday morning as I listened to a sermon on television.

I was in conversation with my best friend and watching a national Christian broadcast when the title of this book and the subject of this chapter fell into my spirit. I heard the whispered words "Get Over It." I began to rejoice and holler in my friend's ear on the phone. "God has just given me the theme and title of this book!!" I then understood why I could not write the first chapter. It was my intention to begin the book by addressing doctrinal teachings and attitudes towards divorce and remarriage. I intended to teach and expound on the scriptures, to address different organizational beliefs and conclude with the statement that each individual had to go to God for their own answers to their particular situation. But this is not what God wanted from me.

There are many books out there to justify or condemn divorce. There are books giving nine steps or twelve steps to a successful marriage. There is an unending amount of material dealing with doctrinal and personal opinions and seminars and retreats dealing with the topics of marriage, separation, and divorce. All of these books, videos, cassettes, etc. may be good in that they have a purpose and hold a wealth of information. The Spirit of the Lord said to me, "I don't need another one of these books from you." People who are already recently separated or divorced don't find comfort in a book that condemns divorce. They may find a wealth of pain in books focusing on marital success. They may learn the mistakes that were made in their marriage. However if they are separated or divorced, these lessons may be too late.

What we need is a word from the Lord that addresses the reality and hurts of separation and divorce. We need a book that addresses the fact that a divorced person is already in the midst of their situation. We are past the point of debating whether divorce is right or wrong. We are past the point of all the successful steps to a well marriage. Our marriages have failed. We stand looking around with our arms wrapped around our waist inwardly crying out in pain, and we ask ourselves, "I am divorced, now what? Do I dry up? Do I shrivel away? Do I hide my head in shame like a leper? How do I go on when my life is a wreck? How do I respond to people who question my salvation because I find myself in the divorced state? Where do I find answers when the church won't even acknowledge my pain, when the church turns a blind eye or is in denial that divorce is a fact of life?" The Spirit said we don't need another book that will discuss God's attitude towards divorce. We need a book that meets the needs of separated and divorced children of God. The book needs to give a message that heals instead of judges.

The simple message that God whispered for me to give you my brothers and my sisters, on that Sunday morning is "GET OVER IT!!!!!" Get over peoples attitudes, doctrinal debates, your hurts, your fears, your disappointments and changes in your social or economic status. Get over man's opinions, lack of forgiveness, rejection, anger and bitterness. Get over low self-esteem, feelings of being stuck and thoughts of committing murder or suicide. Move on with your life.

The term "get over it" can be used to mean many things and

has various levels of severity. We may use this term in anger or in jest. We can speak it to ourselves or to someone else. "Get over it" can mean, give me a break; leave me alone; I don't care what you think; snap out of it; recover; get a grip; survive; let go; or be free. We can say it with an attitude or whisper it under our breath.

So I say to you again, "GET OVER IT!!!" You committed yourself "until death do you part". Well you parted and your spouse is still alive. (No!!! you can't pray for them to die, and you can't throw a banana under their feet!!!) You didn't get married expecting your marriage to fail but since you are divorced, "Get Over It." In other words, recover, get a grip, survive, let go and move on. "Get Over It." Don't be stuck by what others think; or by what other's feel God is saying to you. In order to move on with your life, you may have to tell others to "Get Over It." Leave me alone. Give me a break. I'm not interested in your opinion.

My brothers and my sisters, I have been divorced for over twelve years. I have moved from victim to survivor, from survivor to victor. I became more than a conqueror because I learned how to let go and move on. I turned a deaf ear to opinions and to the voices Satan put into my head. I wrapped myself up in God. Sometimes I had to tell myself "Get Over It." Other times I felt like telling others to "Get Over It" (A.K.A. GET LOST, bleep, bleep, bleep, in Jesus name). I speak to you with the love of Christ, as someone who has shared similar experiences. I speak to you as someone who wants you to move from victim to more than a conqueror. Get Over It by asking God, who is the source of your strength, to heal you and help you to move on with your life.

It is not God's desire for you to live a defeated life because your marriage failed. God desires you to "Get Over It" by finding strength, comfort and direction from Him. He gets no glory out of you living a defeated, bitter, lonely life. He is our loving father. He wants us to live and walk in victory. He has given us the comforter so that we may be comforted. In Matthew 11:28, Jesus said, "Come unto me all ye that labor and are heavy laden and I will give you rest unto your soul." If you have been broken as a result of your failed marriage, the potter wants to put you back together. Satan will do all that he can to convince you to turn your back on God and die spiritually. But Jesus said, " I am come that they might have life, and that more abundantly" (John 10:10). God does not want you to shrivel up and die as a result of your divorce or remarriage. God expects you to "Get Over It" and continue to develop your relationship and service to Him. Like Job, God is cheering and expecting you to be victorious in the end. When God met with His angels, Satan came along. He had been going throughout the earth looking for people to devour and consume. He was the roaring lion on a mission of destruction. Yet, God offered Job up to Satan. It looked like God dropped a dime on Job. He experienced disappointment, loss, and rejection from those he trusted and loved. Because of his love and relationship with God, Job was wise enough to hold on to God. Satan was not successful in getting Job to curse God because Job understood one basic principle, "Shall we accept good from God, and not trouble?" (Job 2:10 NIV). Make no mistake; Job did curse the day he was born. However God, in His infinite love and understanding, gave Job a spiritual pow-pow. He grabbed Job and shook him by the shoulders, "Who is this that darkeneth counsel without knowledge?" In other words, Job, are you giving up because life's circumstances have wrecked your world; or because you've run into unexpected vines of life that are entangling you? Are you going to let them strangle you? I am the omnipotent, omniscient God who you have relationship with. You may not understand what you're going through; but I am God, whom you serve. I've got your back. You were born on purpose, and there is a purpose for everything that you are going through. In other words, God told Job to "Get Over It."

PRAYER

Father God, in the matchless name of Jesus Christ, we first thank you for loving us enough to expose our hidden hurts and hindrances from divorce that have kept us bound. It is so hard to let go of the past failures of our marriage and envision a happy future. We cannot carry or overcome these burdens on our own. Help us, Lord, to GET OVER IT and to move forward with our lives. We realize that you are the source of our strength and our greatest cheerleader. Change our testimony from "God is able" to "look what the Lord has done." With your help, we will loose the chains that bind and soar to our destiny. Amen!!!

Chapter 3

WORSHIP GOD OUT OF YOUR PAIN

Two weeks before my wedding anniversary, my father died. My father had been suffering from cancer. I wanted a miraculous healing but God had something else in mind. Instead of increased pain and suffering from the cancer, God allowed my father to die in peace through an heart attack. Although it was a difficult time, I could still see God's grace in my father's passing. One week after his funeral, I celebrated my wedding anniversary. It was on a weekend. We did not do anything spectacular. I was satisfied just celebrating the survival of one more year. The following weekend was far more memorable. It was the weekend my husband told me he was leaving me and moving out. Although he stated that another woman was not involved, by the end of the next week, he told me he was moving in with the woman who later became his second wife.

I was devastated not only with the fact that my husband left me, but also with the betrayal of his going to another woman. To be truthful, I don't believe he had been having an affair with her. Although I warned him, he never realized that she was chasing after him. Like Sampson, he didn't know what hit him until his hair was cut. After all that we had gone through, I had not expected him to be unfaithful. There had been many problems in our marriage, but up until that time, unfaithfulness was out of the question.

I was heartbroken and still suffering from the loss of my father. I had to find a way to keep myself together. I had two small children who adored their father. They cried every time they saw him or spoke to him on the telephone. I had to hold them as tears ran down all of our faces. For their sakes alone, I had to be strong. I could not afford to fall apart. But God! What was I going to do? How was I going to survive this pain? In Matthew 28:11 Jesus told me to, "Come all ye that labor and are heavy laden." The book of John told me, "Peace I give unto you, not as the world giveth give I unto you." I realized that the only way my children and I would survive was for me to totally trust and lean on God. I had to worship my way out of my pain. I increased my prayer and my praise. Through prayers heavy with pain, I learned to stay before God until He turned tears into laughter, emptiness into hope.

When we experience a loss or rejection, Satan will encourage us to question God, to become angry with God and to blame Him for allowing this painful experience to come upon us. Surely, the God whom we serve would not allow His children to suffer or to be hurt. He should have put cushiony pillows below our feet to keep us from stumbling. Satan whispers into our ear that God must not truly love us. Just as the serpent spoke to Eve and implied that God had a hidden agenda when He told Adam not to eat from the tree of the knowledge of good and evil, he implies that God has fallen down on the job. His goal is to separate us from God, to separate us from the source of our strength. Or like Job, Satan wants us to curse God and die.

Job had to move past the pain of his loss and the pain of not understanding his circumstances in order to hold on to God. Although he could not find God in his circumstances, he was confident that God "knows the way that I take." Like Job, I knew that I could not afford to turn my back on God. If I was going to make it at all, I needed God's help. I increased my church attendance. I became more involved in the auxiliaries I was a part of. I took advantage of every opportunity that arose to worship God. The more I praised God and worshiped Him, the stronger I became.

If you are to overcome being divorced, you cannot focus on the pain, you must focus on the praise. As each day goes by, you will be able to sing, "It's just another day that the Lord has kept me." You will be able to rejoice from the victory of making it one day at a time. One day turns into weeks; weeks turns into months, etc. Then one day you find yourself looking back singing songs of how you survived; songs of how you got over.

PRAYER

Although we don't understand why we are going through the things we are experiencing, we know that you will keep us. In spite of what it looks like or how I feel, I will trust you. I will worship you with my whole heart and withhold nothing. Amen!!!

Chapter 4

SEEN BUT NOT HEARD

The focus of separation or divorce usually is "ME;" What I am going through and what you did to me. But what about the children? I heard a preacher point out that it might not be a coincidence that Jesus addressed children immediately after discussing divorce. The adults noticed the children and began to send them away. But Jesus said, "Suffer little children and forbid them not ..." Why were these children in the presence of adult conversation when they knew this was not allowed? Is it possible that they were drawn to the topic being discussed, because divorce affects the children of the marriage? I won't add to the scripture or imply what the scripture does not. I am only stating that it is interesting to note that the bible lets us know children who were 'seen and not heard' were present when Jesus discussed divorce. We focus on what happens with the parents but do not focus enough on what our children suffer.

We cannot prevent the suffering that our children face. However, we can try to minimize and acknowledge it. Too often our children, are placed in the middle of the parent's struggle. This is not fair to the children and it can damage their entire future. My two children suffered as a result of my divorce. My son suffered the most because he was the oldest child. He also had a "that's my boy" relationship with his father. When their father moved out, there was a physical and emotional distance between them. My son developed Asthma. The accompanying symptoms often left him embarrassed.

Both of my children cried, "I want my daddy!" after visiting their father. I could not ease this kind of pain. I would hold them, as their tears and mine mixed. I asked God to help them and to give me direction. Somewhere, I had learned that children feel they are the cause of their parents' separation. Many times I held my son and told hi, "Daddy didn't leave you, he left me. Your daddy loves you so much." It hurt me to say that his daddy had left me, but it was more important for my son to know that he had not been rejected or abandoned by his father.

Although their father angered me often, I could not let my feelings or actions cause my children additional pain. Too often, parents (yes, even saved parents) use their children as a weapon to punish the other parent. People questioned why I allowed my children to visit their father after he remarried. I answered that I did not have a legitimate reason to keep them from their father. He was not a substance abuser, physically abusive or a whoremonger. Although we did not agree on many things, I had to acknowledge that he loved his children. I also had to consider that my children could grow to resent me for keeping their father from them. Often my decisions were in direct conflict with my emotions. My decisions had to be made based upon what was best for my children and not that I was angry with something their father did, or that I was feeling he was a jerk at that moment. Only God can guide you in times like this. He will help you to make the best decisions for your child/children and help you to keep your emotions out of the decision process.

Too often parents put their children in the middle of their struggles by trying to turn their children against the other parent. They want their children to know "I am right, your other parent is wrong." Truthfully, the other parent may have many problems. However, we must still be careful of turning the child against the other parent. We can plant negative seeds that affect the growth and development of our children. We plant seeds that can affect how they deal with people of the opposite sex when they become adults.

While raising my children, I had to make sure I did not talk negatively about their father. Our children should not know all of the details of the problems between the parents. No matter how angry I became with my children's father, I kept my opinions to myself. I tried not to argue with their father in front of them. This was not always easy. There were a few times when I reacted or snapped an angry statement about their father. But for the most part, I raised my children to love and respect their father. As they grew older, they were able to develop their our attitudes and opinions regarding their father. When they were old enough to understand, I began to discuss with my son only the things he needed to know to help him become a man and not make the same mistakes his father made. I talk with my daughter and share only the things she needs to know to not make the same mistakes I made in choosing a mate. We discuss their issues with their father so that they can be better and not bitter. We discuss forgiveness and understanding so that they maintain a healthy relationship with both of their parents.

One of the hardest decisions I had to make as a parent was to allow my son to live out of state with his father for one year. My children's father's job relocated out of state. Part of his decision to relocate with his job was an agreement I had made to allow my son to live with him the following year. It seemed like a good idea at the time. However, several months before my son was to leave, I had several arguments with his father. Because of my son's age and impressionability, I decided that it would not be a good idea for him to live with his father at that time. The arguments were tremendous. My son could not understand my decision. My children visited their father for the summer months. While there, my son decided he was not coming home. He was sixteen, and he found out that by law, I could not force him to return. My pastor convinced him to come home so that we could discuss and resolve this problem. He came home, but the only resolution he and his father wanted was for him to return to his father.

My son came home bitter, angry and confrontational. The only thing he understood was that his mother had encouraged his father to move thousands of miles away. I had made a promise and was now breaking it. That made his mother a liar. I looked at my son and saw the demonic forces having a field day. I was losing him. Generational curses were trying to take a strong hold on my son. I prayed and talked to my pastor. I made the hardest decision I have ever had to make. For my son's sake, I had to allow him to go to his father. If I had forced him to remain with me, generational curses would have possessed my son. I knew the hazards of sending him away, but I had more to lose by forcing him to stay. My son did experience some losses as a result of this decision. However, today I still have my son. We still have a loving relationship and the generational curse is broken. Now that he is a young adult, we are able to discuss that period of his life. He can now understand why I did not want him to leave home, and why I made the decision to go to his father.

Today there are two necklaces that I wear all the time. I don't take them off because of their preciousness. The first necklace is a gold heart with diamonds and the word MOM written in the middle that I received for Christmas. The second necklace is a diamond cross, given to me for my birthday. They were both given to me by my son, the son I almost lost. God guided me in making the right decision. It was painful and difficult, but I don't regret it. My goal was to protect my seed at all costs.   When it comes to divorce, we must consider our seed. Our children will suffer as a result of the dissolving of the marriage. They also have to make adjustments. They do not understand the circumstances, and they have no control or power. Children of separation or divorce always want their parents to reconcile. If we plan to remarry, we must consider how our children feel about our being with another person, or how they feel about that person. I know people who have waited until their children grew up before they considered remarrying. I also know of situations where the children were made to feel like they were in the way. In choosing a future husband, my children still came first. I cannot bring someone into my life that my children didn't like or can't respect. I also have to watch how the man relates to my children. We will discuss whether or not my children like the man who was trying to date their mother. We also discussed whether they even want their mother to remarry.

Understanding that children want their parents to reconcile, I first talked with my children until they understood there would not be a reconciliation; and that if it was God's will I would remarry.

Both of my children had a period of time where they did not want to consider the possibility of my remarriage. For two years my son threatened to shoot any man looking at his mother. He was very protective. One day, an old high school friend called and I was not at home. My son gave him the third degree and I never got the message that he called. My daughter, on the other hand, wanted me to be happy. Over a period of time, their roles reversed. My son wanted me to remarry because he understood that one day both he and his sister would move out and he did not want me to be alone or lonely. My daughter, on the other hand, did not want to hear "step" anything. There were issues with their stepmother, and she did not want a stepfather. I could not ignore these feelings nor let my daughter's feelings control my relationships. If God sent me a husband at that time, I would have had to reconcile the two. I could not have remarried if my daughter felt threatened or vulnerable. My desires could not overrule protecting the emotions of my child. I always asked her what she thought of the gentleman I was dating. Eventually my daughter became comfortable with the possibility of my remarriage. Now, if I remarry, my children can rejoice with me. We have shared tears of sorrow; we will be able to share tears of joy.

My children and I have shared much during the past twelve years. God helped me and guided me in protecting my seed. Don't forget about your children while caught in the emotion of divorce. They are your precious gift from God. They are your precious seed.

PRAYER

Father God, in the name of Jesus, help us to remember the needs of our children while we go through our separation and divorce. Bless our children, strengthen them and help them to understand and endure the things that they cannot control. Help us as parents to keep our children out of our fights and struggles. Guide us, that we may make the right decisions regarding our children. Amen!!!

Chapter 5

THE ROLLER COASTER LOOP I
(Emotion Battles)

The first weapons the enemy used against me as people learned of my separation from my husband, were the spirits of shame, guilt and embarrassment. They were all powerful emotions that took me to the pit of hell. They suffocated me as I tried to catch my breath from the blows of rejection, abandonment, and loneliness I was already experiencing. I now had to deal with the fact that everyone would know my situation. The seeds that the enemy planted in my mind were thoughts that everyone would know that I was rejected, abandoned, cast aside and worthless. But mostly the seeds that it was my fault my husband left, and that I was a failure as a wife. The enemy made me feel like the women of the old covenant whose husbands publicly denounced them when they divorced.

I was devastated the first time I was confronted by someone who had learned of my situation. We were on our way to an out going church appointment when one of the ministers told me he heard I was separated. While my face remained the same, my heart plummeted, and my mind panicked. "Oh no!" I felt like I had been caught stealing from the benevolence offering. I thought, "They know! Now everyone will know my shame." I felt exposed and vulnerable. My pastor recently asked the question, "What happens when people invade your life because of what happened to you?" This minister had invaded my personal life. I knew this was just the beginning.

Rev. Tina Baker once ministered to me about the masks I wore to cover past pains. I guess at that moment, the mask was on real good. The minister could not tell that I had shrunk two feet inside. Yet, I had to go on. I smiled, sang with the choir, stood up during the sermon and laughed at everyone's jokes. But on the inside, I felt ashamed. I listened as my son told the minister that his father didn't come home anymore. I wished my son would stop talking. He didn't understand or know that I was ashamed and embarrassed. He was just sharing something that he didn't understand, and he needed to talk about it. As much as I didn't feel like I would make it through those initial moments of exposure, God took me through. Although I was often in great pain, God turned my experience into a tool to minister to others. Those initial moments of shame, embarrassment, and guilt were meant for my harm, but God turned it into good. Yes I cried, I often wanted to hide. I often got angry, but God kept me. I survived that which was designed to destroy me. Ultimately, God delivered me and I have been able to help others through their initial moments of separation. I have been able to tap into the emotions that they were wrestling with because I had experienced the same emotions.

In writing this, I want to share with those who are experiencing shame, embarrassment and guilt that these are weapons the enemy is using to try to destroy you. "The thief cometh not, but for to steal, and to kill and to destroy" (John 10:10). If you allow him, the Devil will hold you hostage in guilt and shame. You walk with your head up high on the outside, but you are dragging on the inside. You dread the moment when someone else will inquire about your marital status or asks how your spouse is doing. You feel naked, exposed, and vulnerable. That's just how the Devil wants you to feel. He knows how to magnify these feelings until they overwhelm you. He doesn't let up because you are stumbling. He will even whisper scripture to you. For example, "To be absent from the body is to be present with Christ." He will try to convince you that death is better than life. He intensifies the attack when he knows you are down. Child of God, you are not ignorant of Satan's devices. Your feelings of shame, embarrassment or guilt are not from God. See them as the weapons of mass destruction they are. They are designed to keep you bound and ultimately destroy you.

It amazes me when I think about how the enemy tried to keep me bound by these spirits. The attacks he made didn't always make sense. However, without the strength of God, they could have been effective. During the period of my separation, prior to my divorce, my ex-husband's girlfriend often called my home. She left messages threatening to tell my church members what was going on. Each time I received one of those threats, I would say to myself, "What a stupid threat. What is she going to do, tell my church family that she was living with my husband? Would she eagerly tell the people close to me that she was living in sin with my husband?" They would have taken her straight to the altar. I asked myself what did she expect to happen by sharing this information. Did she expect me to stop fighting the divorce so that I could save face with my church family? The answer to that question was, "Yes". Guilt and shame was supposed to force me to give up the fight. I was supposed to hide in shame, to knuckle under.

The first time I heard those threats, I did panic. However, after awhile the spirit of the Lord lifted me. The Holy Ghost gave me the correct perspective on those attacks. If anyone should have been ashamed or felt guilty, it was the person making the threats. I was able to see past the person threatening to expose my shame and see the strategy of Satan. If I were embarrassed enough, I would leave my church to hide my shame. I would leave the place of safety; the house where I gathered strength, and be fully open to enemy attack. Once the enemy got me to run and hide from my church family, he would keep me running. If I went to another church, he would open a door for my situation to be known, and I would run again.

Without the strength that comes from fellowship with the children of God, I could have been more vulnerable to the attack of Satan. But thanks be to God, for He is the lifter of our heads. He lifts our feelings of shame, embarrassment, and guilt. He exposes these weapons of mass destruction. The more we cling to God, the more we surrender our pain to Him, the stronger we become. Psalms 3 says, "Lord, how are they increased that trouble me! Many are they that rise up against me. Many there be which say of my soul, there is no help for him in God. But thou, O Lord art a shield for me, my glory and the lifter up of mine head." When God lifted up my head, the threats became useless weapons.

I can't stress enough the power of the weapon of guilt that is used against the separated or divorced child of God. There is always the sense of "If I coulda, shoulda, woulda." There must have been something I didn't do that caused my spouse to leave. Unfortunately, in many church environments the woman is made to feel she is lacking if she doesn't meet some mythical standard of the perfect wife. Women go to conferences and seminars where they are advised to just please their husbands in bed and their husbands won't leave. Just cook, clean, greet him with a smile and a negligee, and his eyes won't stray. Therefore, if the husband leaves, the woman feels she has failed in some way. What we are not told, is that there are no absolute guaranteed formulas that will keep your marriage together. A woman can follow all of the instructions. She can do all the things women are taught make a perfect wife, and her husband still leaves her. We need to be taught that these things help, but they do not guarantee a happy marriage. Therefore when a wife finds herself alone, she feels she is lacking and a sense of guilt builds up.

Some church seminars perpetuate her feelings of guilt. Because of her shortcomings, she feels she caused her husband to leave. I went to a seminar at a church convention where the leader of the organization addressed the women. For over an hour he addressed the wife's role in keeping her man happy. She cooks, cleans, lifts his ego and builds his self-esteem. She dressed herself in a way that he will proudly display her on his arm. However, in the bedroom, she's got to know the techniques of a prostitute. The more he spoke, the more battered I felt. The things he said were mostly edifying, but it was the way the information was presented. There was an attitude of, "This is what you are doing wrong, now get it right." Those guilt feelings of "coulda, shoulda, woulda" rose in me. Maybe I should have addressed certain situations differently. Maybe I didn't take enough care of my physical appearance. Maybe I should have cleaned my home more; Maybe, maybe, maybe. For over an hour, we were told we were inadequate. We needed to get ourselves together. We were told what we were not doing to keep our man satisfied; and this is why he will leave or has already left.

In one sentence, at the end of this tirade, he concluded with the statement, "Of course you can do all these things, and he still leave." I thought to myself, "What a difference his presentation would have made if he had opened up with that statement. Or, if he had at least stated that these were suggestions not guarantees. What a difference his presentation would have made if he had not been crushing the spirits of the women but encouraging them." I entered that seminar eager and light hearted. After all, daddy was going to talk to his daughters. I left that seminar feeling beaten, broken, inadequate and guilty. I tried to smile as I held back tears. Even as I write this, the pain of that moment brings tears to my eyes. I left the seminar and walked over to a friend. I told her that I felt beaten up, like a steamroller had just rolled over me.

How many other women left that seminar feeling as I did? Even worse, how many left believing the hype? How many women who were already dealing with feelings of guilt left the seminar more bruised and broken? How many left believing that if they went home and became the "perfect wife," their marriage would be saved? The saving grace for me was that the Holy Ghost would not allow those seeds to take root in my spirit. I've learned that we don't have to accept everything that Satan throws at us. Yes, I said Satan. Although it was a church leader making the statements, much of what he said came from his own attitude towards women and marriage. His words tore down rather than built up the character of women. God always builds up. If God corrects, it is with love and a presentation that will encourage growth and change rather than criticism. Although some of the information was correct with regards to ways to build a marriage, it was presented from an accusatory perspective. It was presented in a manner which tore down self-esteem and as if the presenter was correcting an errant child. That attitude was not of God.

Although I felt beaten and bruised, God would not allow those seeds to take root in my spirit. He continued to whisper to me, "This is not correct for your situation." However, while God spoke to me, Satan also spoke to me. While the Holy Ghost dried up the seeds sown by the presider's words, Satan began to plant other seeds. It is important to know what voice is speaking to you. The spirits of anger and resentment rose up within me creating stony ground for any future seeds to be planted by this man. I refused to accept that the only way, to keep a husband was to become his doormat. Anger and resentment not only killed any remaining seeds sown by this leader, but they also caused me to reject his leadership. I developed the attitude that there was nothing he could teach me. I could acknowledge that he was an anointed preacher, but every time I saw him, I became angry. Righteous anger or indignation as a result of an injustice is acceptable. But be careful Satan doesn't use anger as a weapon against you. The spirit of anger brought on the spirits of resentment, rebellion, and rejection. I resented what the presider said. I rejected what he said, I then rebelled again him. These attitudes and actions opened the door for the spirits of bitterness and hatred to enter. I found the seeds of bitterness taking root, and I became angrier every time I saw him.

When the Holy Ghost revealed to me that I was beginning to hate this man, I had to catch myself and check my attitude. I had to repent and ask God for help. God allowed me to clearly see the spiritual battle I was in. Although this leader did not know me personally, his words were like a personal attack, and I fought back with resentment and anger. Bitterness crept in so that every time I saw this leader I felt bitterness and, then hatred towards him. God had to deliver me. I had to learn to forgive this leader for the hurt that he did not know he caused. I didn't have to agree with his teaching in order to forgive him. As I began to forgive him of his offense, the spirit of bitterness was released. I was no longer angry with this leader. I saw him as a leader who needed to be delivered from his own demons.

Forgiveness was essential to my healing and deliverance. Jesus taught His disciples about the importance of forgiveness. He understood that the lack of forgiveness keeps us bound and prevents our growth. The inability to forgive is a spirit that keeps the offense in the present tense. A lack of forgiveness and bitterness go hand in hand and poison the soul of the person. Because they keep the offense always in the present, the person is not able to heal. The wound is kept open, and infection sets in. This is how bitterness was turning into hatred. When I forgave this leader, my wound was cleaned. The infection of hatred was removed, and I was able to heal.

Although I was healing from the wound of that experience, I was still bound by guilt and shame. I was still meeting people whom I had not seen in a long time who did not know of my divorce. When explaining my marital state, I still felt pain. I still felt ashamed and often was made to feel guilty.

One of the things that happen when people invade your life because of what happened to you is that they make assumptions and judgments without correct information. They take one fact and run with it. One of the reasons the spirit of guilt was a stronghold in my life was my response to the assumptions some people made regarding my separation and divorce. Unfortunately, in the church, it is often assumed that it is the wife's fault when a couple separates or divorces. On one occasion I was having a conversation with a sister I had not seen for several years. When I told her I was not with my husband, she said, "You church women" and shook her head (Did you notice I said she was a church woman?) She assumed that I had been self-righteous and put my husband out because he was not saved. She didn't know that neither my husband nor I had been saved when we married. When I explained to her that my husband left me and was living with another woman, all she said was, "Oh." I realize some women in ignorance beat their unsaved husbands with the Word of God. But why do people assume that all saved women with unsaved husbands are self-righteous? It is a stereotype and a weapon used against women who are separated or divorced. We must always explain that we did not push our spouse away. We must proclaim our innocence. We are presumed guilty until proven innocent. Because of this, the enemy is able to whisper that there was something we could have done or didn't do that caused our spouses to leave.

On another occasion, I was having a discussion with a minister friend in an administrative office at a convention. We were laughing and talking about simple things. I'd just bought a white "missionary" hat that had three beads hanging off the side. My friend didn't like the hat. He thought it was too flamboyant to be a "missionary" hat. There was a woman in the room who he called over to ask her opinion. Of course, she didn't find anything wrong with my hat. I began to tease my friend for his stuffiness. I don't remember how the subject turned to our marital status. However, we both told this woman that we were divorced. Her attitude immediately changed. All of a sudden we were in a walk-in freezer. By her attitude, I realized she had assumed we had both divorced so that we could be together. She assumed we were a couple. I found myself to this stranger that my husband had left me. I explained that if it had been my choice, I would have still been married. I found myself telling her that he was living with another woman and contrary to what she thought, I had fought the divorce. Of course, I now realize I could have told her it was none of her business. However at the time, I felt obligated and pressured to declare my innocence. My friend and I laughed after the woman left. We knew that we had not presented ourselves as a couple. In fact, I was noticeably several years older than him. Although we laughed, the situation was not funny. We both understood that people make assumptions when you state that you are divorced. In the church, the assumption for a woman is that she was self-righteous, she didn't take care of her outward appearance or she didn't fulfill her wifely duties. In a few instances, it will be assumed that she left her husband for another man. The assumption for a separated or divorced man in the church is that he was unfaithful and left his wife for another woman, or that he was too involved in his ministry. Whatever the assumption, you always feel guilty until you can prove otherwise.

I know I have only addressed separation and divorce from the perspective of the person whose spouse left them. However there are situations where a child of God may find herself of himself in a position where they are the initiator of the separation or divorce. In too many churches, they are not considered guilty until proven innocent. They are presumed guilty, guilty, guilty! Because some Christians consider divorce a sin, the child of God who initiated the divorce is considered guilty of sin. He or she becomes bound by the shame and guilt associated with sin.

The child of God who is abused, whose spouse was unfaithful, or who married for all the wrong reasons may be stuck within a marriage that is sucking all of the life and spirit out of them. They may have prayed and been led of the Lord to separate or divorce. God may have released them from the marriage, but they are not released by the church members. The person may remain within the marriage to please other people, and resentment builds up. If they follow the leading of the Lord, they face criticism and judgments from their church members and friends.

I have a friend whose husband became an alcoholic. After several years of praying and trying to make the marriage work God, released her from the marriage. She was forced to ask him to leave the home. Not only did he become a substance abuser, but he also became a womanizer. The decision my friend made was very difficult and painful. She had to weigh the effects of the separation and divorce on her family. Although she had not made this decision lightly, she was made to feel guilty by the Christian friends she had expected to support her. Because of her feelings of shame regarding her failed marriage, she had not shared her decision with her friends for several months. Finally she revealed her decision to two minister friends of hers. These ministers literally harassed her for years regarding this decision. She was encouraged to take her husband back and continue to pray for him. Although there was no change in her husband, she was supposed to take him back and expect God to miraculously turn him around. If God had not done this work within the years she had been praying, what made these ministers feel God was now going to make a move? It was also suggested that the problem could be a lack of her performance in her bedroom. She was told that she was being brainwashed by Christians who had moved outside of God's will because they approved of divorce and remarriage. Even her pastor was being criticized for brainwashing her into thinking she could get divorced.

As God would release her from guilt and reassure her that she was making the correct decision, these friends would put her back into bondage by pressuring her and telling her she was out of the will of God. Although she never agreed to take her husband back, she questioned her own judgment and the voice of God within her life. By rejecting her decision, these ministers implied that they had a better relationship with God. They knew God's will for her life better than she or her pastor did. Once these friends accepted that she was going to follow through with the divorce, they them pressured her not to remarry. They did not want her to go to hell by disobeying God. After two years of being harassed by these friends, she informed them that she not only would divorce her husband, but should the opportunity arise, she would remarry. They could either accept or reject her decision, but she would obey the voice of God in her life rather than the voice of man.

I was angry at the boldness and arrogance of these ministers. They had judged my friend and found her to be in sin because she was divorcing her husband. When I consider my friend's situation, I cannot remain angry with her minister friends. Like the friends of Job, they felt they were helping her. Jobs friends counseled him from the "present truth" of their day. (Although God does not change, man's understanding of His ways and His word change. This is called present truth). In Job's day, the only reason a man suffered as Job did was because he was being punished for sin. Job's friends wanted him to repent and get back into fellowship with God. In the same way, these ministers addressed divorce and remarriage from their current frame of reference. They had been taught for years that divorce was sin. Scripture was given to back up this principle. Although many Christians are rethinking the teachings on divorce and remarriage, these ministers were stuck in the "present truth" of their day. While I use the word harass, they would have considered themselves as helping or restoring. They did not mean to harm or hurt their friend. They had good intentions. However their words caused my friend to experience guilt. To these ministers, there had to be another way to solve her marital problem. They implied there was something she had not done that caused her husband to become an alcoholic and womanizer. Or she was not trusting God enough, or praying enough for God to deliver. The guilt she was made to feel, kept her from taking the steps necessary to finalize her divorce. The assumptions and presumptions of these minister friends watered the seeds of guilt and shame.

We must understand that whichever side of the divorce table the child of God finds himself/herself; they can be attacked by the spirit of guilt. It is not easy to overcome this spirit. It may take more than one deliverance experience. Counseling could also be necessary for total deliverance. If we are to survive and move on with our lives, we must be delivered from this spirit and the spirit of shame associated with guilt.

I had two experiences I had that caused the strongholds of guilt and shamed related to being divorced to be broken. The second experience I will address in the next chapter. The first experience was a church organization convention. I knew that when I returned home from this convention, my husband was going back into court to serve me a new set of divorce papers. The first set had been improperly served, and he was forced to withdraw them. My spirit was broken, and I was seeking God for help. The missionary department had a seminar on separation and divorce. I was tired of hurting, and I had hoped that this seminar would give me some relief. I was amazed by the number of women attending this seminar. There were so many other women struggling with the pain of a failed marriage.

The facilitator of the seminar was a divorced woman who had been kept by God for thirty years. She explained that it did not matter what caused us to be in the state of separation or divorce. It didn't matter whether it was our fault or not; whether we were the initiator or the recipient of divorce papers, we were all in the same situation, alone. The key was that even if it was our fault, we could learn from our mistakes and move on. Our lives didn't end because we made mistakes. Our mistakes could become stepping-stones for our future. Our lives didn't end because we were abandoned by our spouses, or because we had to make the decision to end our marriage. DIVORCE HAPPENS. Some of us had to deal with situations beyond our control. Some of us were abused; we were the victims of physical or emotional abuse.

The facilitator made us look at our situations from a different perspective. Her personal testimony was one of a woman who had done every thing to please her unsaved husband. She followed all the rules, yet she still found herself alone. She cooked, cleaned, pampered, obeyed, dressed up, dressed down and she stayed at home when he told her to. She even accompanied him to bars. Now some may question that last item. Some may say she was out of the will of God because she went into a bar. Some may even suggest that this was the reason God did not save her marriage, or deliver her husband. We can have opinions about her choice, however, she did every thing she knew how to do to save her marriage and to please her husband. Yet, he still left her. He told her that he just didn't want a saved wife.

Because of her testimony, I realized there are no set formulas to guarantee the survival of a marriage. There would always be moments when I look back and question my actions, but I don't have to feel guilty about them. Whether we made negative decisions in the past we still had to go on. Divorce and separation happen because of decisions our spouses or we make. We can make poor choices and we cannot control the choices of our spouses. I realized that although our marriage may have ended but our lived didn't. We are still living, breathing individuals. We could choose to be bound by our past or feelings of guilt from our failed marriages or we could make a positive decision to be free. I chose at that moment to be free. The seed of hope and the spirit of peace began to be nurtured in my soul.

I realize there will always be moments in my past that I will feel I should have lived differently. However, I can now look back without feeling guilty. I often felt guilty wondering if I should have stayed home more. Every conference, every seminar, and sermon discussing married relationships seemed to emphasize the need to stay home with your spouse, especially if your unsaved spouse commented on how often you went to church. Through the years, I have learned, the division the enemy causes within a marriage by this issue. The enemy made me feel guilty wondering if my marriage would have been saved if I had stayed home more. Was I guilty of being insensitive to my husband's need to spend time with his wife?

I am now sure there were times when I should have stayed home. But during the time I was living the experience, I was doing the best I knew to do to survive. Hindsight is always 20/20. However, when you are in the midst of the situation, your vision is cloudy. I was fighting for my mental, emotional, and, spiritual survival. When I came to church, I hid in the secret place of God. I found emotional safety and peace. I once told my pastor that I was coming to Refuge Church for refuge. I gained strength face the next battle. Due to my circumstances, I did not feel that I was endangering my marriage by going to church several days a week. When I was home, my husband and I did not spend quality time together. I watched television, listened to music, or read a book while he spent hours writing and playing music. Anyway when I stayed home, I was usually alone, so I chose to go to church where I could freely worship God and find peace.

I did not know that people judged my life by how often I attended church. I did not feel guilty about my church activities until I found that some of my church members did not consider me a good wife because of how often I came to church. Prior to attending my current church, I had been saved for eight years. I left my home church at my husband's request. I had been actively involved in several auxiliaries and was a leader in our youth ministry. Yet, I left my church because I felt it was the will of God to ensure my husband's salvation. However, after being a member of my current church for two years, I felt I did not fully fit in. I tried to be a part of the youth department. I was 27 years old and had a 2 and1/2 year old son, but I would still have been considered a part of the youth department at my former church. Some of the members of the youth department of my new church accepted me, but others didn't. One evening I asked one of the youth why I was not accepted. He stated, "They feel you should be home with your husband." I was floored. I had not expected that answer.

People who had not taken the time to know me, who didn't know my circumstances, had weighed me in the balance and found me wanting. People who did not know the struggles or sacrifices I had made during the eight years of my marriage before coming to that church, had decided that I needed to be at home. In their eyes, I was not a good wife. They did not know that the work I did in the church kept me grounded and from giving up. No one asked whether my husband wanted to do things with me. Neither did they know that the early years of my marriage caused me to run God. They only knew that I was a wife, and wives stay home. The people from my former church who knew me understood my circumstances. They never questioned my church attendance. Now for the first time, I was made to feel guilty about going to church. The root cause of this feeling of guilt came from the very place I sought peace. The seed of guilt was planted. (A good wife stays home regardless of her circumstances. Therefore, I was not being a good wife every time I left the house, and I questioned whether this was the right thing to do.)

Every seminar I attended after my husband and I separated made me feel like I had caused him to leave by not being a good wife. I had to fight to keep the seeds of guilt from taking root. It was at this missionary seminar that I was delivered from the guilt related to this issue. The first thing I accepted was that there was no guarantee that if I had stayed home, my marriage would have been saved. The problems within my marriage began long before I attended church. As I previously stated, my married drove me to Christ.

Not only did I realize my staying at home would not have changed the outcome of my marriage. But I also accepted that if my state of separation had been the result of my actions, I still had to pull my life together and move on. It doesn't matter what led to an individuals state of separation or divorce as long as we learn from whatever mistakes we made and move forward with our future. Learning from these mistakes may result in reconciliation. But if not, move on! I learned that there were things I contributed to my husband's decision to leave. I chose to let them be stepping stones rather than stumbling blocks. At this missionary seminar, God released me from certain feelings of guilt and empowered me to look at my future with a positive attitude. I don't intend to repeat the mistakes I made in my past marriage when I remarry.

The key in my release was understanding that I had done the best that I knew how to do. My decisions were based upon my survival and determination to let nothing separate me from God. The areas that I now have a better understanding of will direct my actions in the future. I can regret past mistakes, however, I don't have to be bound by them. As the saying goes, "Don't cry over spilled milk." The implication is that, one should just clean it up and move on. Child of God, you don't have to be bound by the spirit of guilt for past mistakes. You don't have to be bound by feelings of guilt imposed by others. We cannot undo our past. We can only learn from it and grow from it. We cannot control the choices made by others, we can only control our own decisions.

Children of God do find themselves separated or divorced. However, it is not God's will for them to be bound by shame, embarrassment or guilt. "Whom the son has set free is free indeed." When God has set you free, you cannot allow yourself to be tangled again into the yoke of bondage. The Devil will try to bring the spirit of guilt back upon you. There will always be reminders that will connect you with the issues of your past. The enemy will try to replant the seeds of guilt. They will try to take root again. But let them fall on fallow ground. Don't water it, don't nurture it and the seeds of guilt will die.

Although I was delivered from feelings of guilt imposed by people outside of my marriage, I was still bound by feelings of guilt as a result of my relationship with my husband. There were also hidden emotions that were the result of my separation and divorce. The experience that released me from these feelings of guilt also exposed and released me from emotions and strongholds that were hidden even from me. The mask that I wore for the saints of God and my family and my friends was also convincing me that I was emotionally and spiritually whole. However, God who in His infinite love, forces us to face ourselves and the hidden issues we want to ignore, extended His grace towards me. He forced me to face the dark things in my life that Satan was using to bind me and keep me from reaching my full potential in Christ (and in future relationships).

Chapter 6

THE ROLLER COASTER LOOP II (Wrestling)

The chain of events that occurred after the judge granted my husband the divorce had me in an emotional roller coaster that I refused to acknowledge. One February, I met a man that I liked. My relationship with this man was a part of the process that helped rebuild my self-esteem. We were only friends at the time. I did not consider the relationship becoming more than friends because my church did not believe in divorce and remarriage. In addition I was still holding on to the possibility that God would restore my marriage. One day my children asked me if their father could move in with us because he was leaving the woman he was living with and needed a temporary place to stay. Although we were no longer married, I allowed him to return to my home. We were not attempting to reconcile, even though my children and I had hopes. While residing in my home, he decided to reconcile and marry the other woman.

The day she picked him up from my home was the closest I had ever come to jumping on her and giving her the beat down her actions deserved. My children stood next to me crying. I pushed my own feelings aside to minister to my children. Everyday I went through the motions of living and with thoughts of spending my entire future alone. Even though I had a friend, I could not consider marrying him. For my children's sake and because of the mask I wore for the world, I kept my feelings hidden. It was "Hallelujah anyhow." In May, when they married, I said "Hallelujah anyhow." In June, when she left a telephone message on my phone informing me of her pregnancy, I still said "Hallelujah anyhow." Make no mistake, I did not have victory over my emotions. I just buried them. I was in a comfort zone living life like a martyr. However, God had other plans for me. He didn't need me to be a martyr. He needed me to be whole and complete.

In August, I went to the church convention in West Virginia. I was sharing a room with a friend from my church, her mother and grandmother. We arrived on Friday afternoon. That evening, we went to the worship service. The service was uplifting, and I rejoiced in the Lord. But immediately after the service, as we went to our room, depression fell on me like a ten-ton weight. I found myself wanting to cry. I needed to be alone. There was a river that flowed behind the hotel. I went to the room with my friends and immediately found a reason to leave. I found myself walking along the walkway beside the river. Tears flowed, but I didn't understand why. I walked and sang songs of worship, but the spirit of depression did not leave. After about an hour, I returned to the room. I asked God what was wrong with me. There was no answer. For the next three days, I had the same experience. During the day, I attended seminars and business sessions. I fellowshipped, laughed, and enjoyed myself. I rejoiced while in the presence of thousands of spirit filled believers. The convention was always an awesome time for me. Yet each night after the evening worship service, I found myself walking the streets engulfed in depression. Ultimately, each night I ended up at the river, trying to sing songs of worship to lift my spirit. I told God this did not make sense. I loved Him so much, yet I wasn't finding peace in my usual place of Refuge. I felt alone and broken. Tears flowed and I questioned what was going on.

Finally, on Monday evening as I walked along the side of the river, God spoke one soft whisper, "Tonight, we wrestle!" Suddenly it all became clear. Immediately, I understood the magnitude of God's love towards me. This roller coaster of emotions I had been experiencing was orchestrated by God to wrestle hurts out of my life. Those three words He whispered to me were the topic of a sermon preached at my church a few years prior. "Tonight, we wrestle" Those few words opened the floodgates to emotions I had not dealt with. I thought of the significance of their meaning. A key point of the sermon was that when the angel asked Jacob his name, Jacob was forced to face the root of his greatest pain, the thing he wanted most to hide. As the minister preached, he gave various scenarios of painful past experiences. After each scenario, he would ask the question, "What else is wrong with you?" Layer by layer, God exposed hidden pains in each person's life. The angel wrestled with Jacob, exposing what affected and hindered Jacob the most. Then the angel blessed him turning his situation around and taking the sting and pain out of the circumstances of his past. The angel then gave Jacob a new name, Israel (One who has contended with God).

When God spoke those three words to me, everything stopped. He exposed the source of my pain and said, "Tonight, Justine we wrestle!" He revealed to me that I had not been dealing with my feelings regarding my divorce, my ex-husband's remarriage or his new wife's pregnancy. He showed me myself, as I went through the motions with a straight faced smile. Oh it was "Hallelujah anyhow." "How are you feeling Justine?" "Oh, I'm fine; blessed of the Lord." God said, "No, you are not fine! You have not dealt with these issues. But tonight, we wrestle." I could fool everyone else, even myself, but God said, "You don't fool me. You have to deal with these issues. So...Tonight, we wrestle!"

I was so grateful to God because He loved me enough to show me myself. I held onto those words. God was wrestling things out of me for my good. He was turning my attitude around, exposing wounds that began to heal instantly. The blood ceased to flow; skin tissues began to grow. I began to realize there were wounds that still needed to be exposed to the air to eventually grow a scab. There were also deeper scars that had scabs but were not healing on the inside. God let me know that He was giving me total healing. However healing did not happen overnight. I could not overcome the pain of my yesterday as long as I was not allowing wounds to heal. Deep wounds take time to heal and God was dealing with deep wounds.

When God tells you "Tonight, we wrestle," your tonight can

last one night, one year or even longer. God's time is not our time. Although weeping may endure for a night and joy comes in the morning, your night may be an Alaskan night. You only know that joy will eventually come. My wrestling night with God lasted from August to October. I had to acknowledge that I was hurting, I was angry, and feelings of rejection were once again trying to become a stronghold. Feelings of being unlovable and feelings of guilt were taking root. But I had pretended they did not exist. God, with one sentence exposed it all. However, full deliverance took place several months after God exposed the wound.

My church was in revival with a dynamic young preacher from North Carolina. I had never heard him preach before, and he has not been back to my church since then. In his preaching style, he ministered to a few people after each sermon. When he finished ministering, he would ask them how they felt and whether they had received what they were looking for from the Lord. If they responded that they had received their blessing, he would make the statement, "Don't fool me now." Although I don't remember the topic of his sermon, the message caused me to reflect on what I was going through as a result of my marriage and divorce. God was still wrestling with me, and He intensified the struggle. It was time to be fully delivered. I told God I didn't want to be bound by the feelings that were keeping me from being the woman of God He called me to be. It was making me insecure. I didn't want to continue feeling like a failure as a woman.

I stood on the prayer line opening myself up for spiritual release. I worshiped God and talked to Him as I waited for my turn to be prayer for. Finally, I stood before the Man of God. My moment of deliverance had come. I stood in anticipation. The man of God laid hands upon my head but he did not address the issues I had been discussing with God. He ministered to me words that brought joy in other areas of my life. However I was still bound. I walked away praising God but unfulfilled. I questioned God. I was disappointed with Him. God knew what I needed; yet He had not used the man of God to deliver me. I didn't realize God was still wrestling with me.

The man of God continued to pray for people. When he

finished, he once again began to ask people how they felt. One after another people responded that God had met their need. They had received their blessing. Occasionally, he would make his statement, "Don't fool me now." He looked at me and asked me if I had received what I wanted from the Lord. I smiled and shook my head, "Yes'. The mask was up. The hallelujah anyhow face and attitude was settling for less than my total deliverance. But then the man of God stated the fateful statement, "Don't fool me now." Something inside of me broke. I wanted to be free. I had not received what I needed from the Lord. "Don't fool me now." That's what I was trying to do, deceive everyone around me into thinking I had everything together. I was fine. That voice from August whispered, "You are not fine. Don't fool me now." Who was I trying to fool, certainly not God! I believed God enough to expect Him to use this man of God, but I was not being truthful. I knew God had the power to deliver me, and the knowledge of what was hindering my life. He knew the inner me. He knew I was not whole. God knew I was sitting there disappointed and bound. So why was I telling this man of God, His servant that I had received what I needed from God? Why was I wearing the mask of satisfaction?

God wrestled the answers out of me. I was concerned with what others would think. God forbid that my brothers and sisters learned that I didn't have it all together; I had hidden issues, or that I was not the perfect child of God. At that moment, in a few seconds God said, "Make a decision." Why should I be bound, when He wanted me to be delivered? The issue was; how badly did I want to be delivered. Would I be willing to let down the mask and expose my vulnerability? For the first time, with boldness I didn't know I had and with honesty, I let down the mask. I looked at the minister and told him I had not received what I wanted from the Lord. If the man of God had not made the statement, "Don't fool me now"; I would have accepted defeat. But in spite of the mask, I desperately wanted to be whole and completely delivered. I stood up and walked back into the center isle.

I explained that I had come onto the prayer line to deal with my divorce and husband's remarriage. The man of God's next words opened the floodgates. "God said it is not your fault. You have done all that you could do." Although the man of God said more, those words were the only words I heard. I was on the verge of release. God was no longer wrestling with me. He was giving me a new name, a new identity. "You shall now be called 'Not guilty.'" The dam in my spirit broke. I began to cry the unsightly tears of one who is being released from torment. August to October God wrestled with me. Now I was free with a new identity. Even as God released me, I knew that the victory had not come only through the words spoken by the man of God. Freedom came as a result of my being honest with God, myself and with man. My pain and feelings of guilt were hidden in darkness. By stepping forward when the minister said, "Don't fool me now." I exposed this dark area of my life. Because it was hidden in darkness, Satan had free reign to keep me bound. Now that this darkness in my life was exposed, God could heal me. Prior to that moment, other people had told me that my circumstance was not my fault. I even told myself that I had done all I could do, or at least I had done the best I knew how to do. But when the words came from God, I was instantaneously set free.

Those words released me from the recurring feelings of anger and guilt that the enemy tried to bring back into my life as a result of other people's attitudes. It also released me from the feelings of guilt and failure that I had been made to feel during my thirteen years of marriage. I had experienced thirteen years of an emotionally abusive marriage where I was made to feel like every negative thing that happened was my fault. I was lacking in so many areas that I was not a good wife or mother.

Just as the angel's question to Jacob went to the root of the center of his pain, those words from God went to the root of what kept me bound by feelings of condemnation and failure. The angel wrestled with Jacob long enough for Jacob to realize the angel was the source of his blessing. Jacob's battle changed from the angel wrestling with Jacob, to Jacob wrestling with the angel. Once Jacob realized what he wanted from God, he would not let go until he received his blessing. God wrestled with me from August until that fateful night when I realized deliverance was at hand. I then began to wrestle with God. I would not leave that service the same way I came in.

God loved me enough to force me to face the ugly, hidden things that were binding my life. Once He forced me to face my demons, I had to determine whether or not I wanted to be delivered. Because I had not received deliverance the first time I went onto the prayer line, I had to continue to wrestle with God. When the man of God spoke to me the second time, I had to answer two questions. When do you want your blessing, and how badly do you want to be delivered? Did I want to be free badly enough to expose myself and make myself vulnerable? Was I more concerned with what others would think of me than with being set free? Although I had not received what I wanted, God was giving me another chance to be delivered. But, how badly did I want it? Was I going to sit there disappointed but wearing the face of satisfaction, or was I going to face the truth? Those words; "Don't fool me now," pushed me to change my circumstances from God wrestling with me to me holding on to God until He blessed me.

"How badly do you want it?" I wanted to be delivered badly enough to take off the mask and expose myself. I wanted it enough to risk being judged by my brothers and sisters. The words spoken to me broke the chains of bondage. The Lord said, "It was not your fault, you have done all that you could do." The weight lifted. Although I had heard these words before, they had not brought deliverance. It was the act of exposing my hidden shame, of dropping the mask and facing my demons that opened the door of deliverance. I found myself no longer feeling hurt or angry because my ex-husband remarried, or that they were having a child. Although I tried to pinpoint the moment of this healing, I now realize it was on that night when God allowed me to wrestle with Him. Like Jacob, I was one who contended with God and lived.

The second question I faced that night was, "When do you want to be delivered?" Just as important as the question of, "How badly do you want to be delivered, is the question of when do you want to be delivered?" If we have not made up our minds to be free, we will continue to suffer in bondage. When we pray with a person to receive the Holy Ghost, we ask the question, "When do you want to receive the Holy Ghost?" If the person does not say he /she wants to receive it at that moment, they usually will not receive it when we pray with them. They are not ready to let go of everything. In the Old Testament, Moses asked Pharaoh when he wanted a specific plague to end. Pharaoh's reply was the next day. The plague ended the next day. However, Pharaoh could have asked for the plague to end the same day, or at that moment. God would have immediately brought deliverance. By going on the prayer line that night, I was determined to be free right then. But that didn't happen. I sat in my seat accepting defeat; deliverance would not be coming that night. When the man of God said, "Don't fool me now" I became more determined to be delivered right then. This required me to let go and allow God to minister to me, to reach into my battered, broken heart in order to heal and be restored. I could not be concerned with who saw my pain, or my brokenness. In answer to the question; "How badly did I want to be delivered?" badly enough to expose myself. In answer to the question, "When did I want to be delivered?" Now!

My brothers and sisters there are things God wants to wrestle out of you. God may not require you to expose yourself to others, but He does require you to be open and honest with Him. Those emotions that you are keeping hidden in darkness are preventing you from being free and from moving on with your life. You can choose to hide behind a mask, or you can choose to wrestle with God. The questions are when do you want to be free and how badly do you want it?

Chapter 7

——◆——

THE ROLLER COASTER THE FINAL LOOP

In one night, in a moment, my life was changed. Chains fell, the burden was lifted and I was free to move on with my life. I was on the way to becoming the woman of God I am called to be. The sense of failure and the weight of guilt surrounding my marriage and divorce totally lifted. God was now able to deal with other emotional areas of my life. Over the next two years, God revealed to me strongholds, emotional hindrances or phases that a person goes through as a result of separation or divorce. Each of these things has to be overcome in order to successfully have a relationship with a new person. The separated or divorced person may experience any combination of the following emotions that are stumbling blocks and can become strongholds: lack of forgiveness, bitterness, lack of self-esteem, fear and withdrawal, and questioning of your judgment. While I did not experience withdrawal, God allowed me to see these strongholds in other separated or divorced people.

Lack of forgiveness and bitterness are two of the most obvious of the emotions to detect. The person who angrily says, "I will never remarry" needs to examine himself/herself for unforgiveness and bitterness. They feel abandoned, rejected and violated by their spouse. They think to themselves; "I can't believe this person did this to me." It is easy for someone to tell a person to let go of hurts and forgive their ex-spouses. It is far more difficult for that person to actually to do. Yet, if you are going to be whole, if you want to stay in right fellowship with God, you must learn to forgive your ex-spouse of whatever the offense. "Forgive us our trespasses, as we forgive those who trespass against us."

I had to constantly examine myself, as I often had experiences that I had to let go of in order to keep unforgiveness from taking root. I told God on several occasions that I did not want to be friends with my ex-husband. I often had to catch the tone of my voice. However, I also knew that if I did not forgive him, I would make hell my home. I asked myself was the offense worth it to lose God or my place in God? Therefore I made forgiveness a priority. We must understand the control a lack of forgiveness has on our lives. The lack of forgiveness leads to bitterness. These two spirits (unforgiveness and bitterness) are strong spirits that keep the offense in the present tense. It could be ten or fifteen years later, however, if the lack of forgiveness or bitterness have set in; the person will feel just as hurt as when the offense first occurred.

The lack of forgiveness and bitterness will cause the person to withdraw with the intension of never allowing themselves to be vulnerable again. We mentally tell ourselves that, "My spouse hurt me, so I will not open myself up to allow someone else to hurt me." The harm and hindrance of this attitude is that we become so guarded that even if God sent someone into their life, we would reject that person. Even harder to deal with is the situation wherein it is God's plan for the couple to reconcile. The person says in their mind "After what my spouse did to me, God you want me to take them back? I don't think so! God you must have lost your mind!" The lack of forgiveness and bitterness will cause a person to reject God's will for them.

In either scenario, God would have to deliver his child before He could bless them. The lack of forgiveness and bitterness therefore hinders our own growth and keeps us bound. Although these emotions are not exclusive to separated or divorced people. They are intensified by the fact that the person entrusted themselves to their spouse. They made a pledge to each other, they committed themselves until "death do us part." That trust was violated.

Fortunately for me, a lack of forgiveness never turned into bitterness causing me to not want to deal with men at all. Once God told me that marriage was in my future, I could not turn my back on the thought of remarrying. I had moments of unforgiveness and moments of bitterness. However, God did not allow those emotions to take root. Although I did tell God that I did not want to be friends with my ex-husband, God reminded me that if I did not forgive my ex-husband, God could not forgive me. "Forgive us our trespasses as WE FORGIVE those who trespass against us." YES! God did remind me that the lack of forgiveness would cause me to have my part in the LAKE OF FIRE. I quickly learned to fight my own flesh and forgive the past offenses my ex-husband did to me.

Forgiveness didn't mean I did not feel hurt, nor did it stop me from getting angry about new offenses. Just like we have to take one day at a time, we have to overcome each new offense, one offense at a time. Eventually the hurt disappears, the offense falls into the past, and you can move on with your life. I can now say, "Thank you for leaving me. You actually set me free. Satan meant it for my harm, but GOD!!!"

PRAYER

Father God, in the name of Jesus Christ. help us to overcome and be delivered from all the emotions tied to separation and divorce that keep us bound. Lord, wrestle with us until we expose the darkness behind our masks. Wrestle with us until we are forced to deal with the hurts that we have tried to ignore and hide even from ourselves. Lord makes us emotionally whole so that we can fulfill our destiny. Amen!!!

Chapter 8

GOD'S PROMISE

One Saturday evening, as I drove to prayer, I questioned God. Why do the heathen reign? Why does it seem like the unjust can do whatever they want and seem to be blessed? Here I was, the 'saved' one, but my ex-husband seemed to be the one prospering. "God," I asked, "What will happen to me?" I was having a pity party. Life just didn't seem fair.

I arrived at the church and waited for prayer to start. As the minister led us to go onto our knees to pray, I could not begin to pray. After a moment, God led me to read the Bible. God had often led me to a specific scripture before or after I prayed. I opened my bible and continued to turn the pages until I came to Isaiah 62:1-5. Verses two and four leaped out at me. " And the Gentile shall see thy righteousness, and all kings thy glory: and thou shall be called by a new name, which the mouth of the Lord shall name...Thou shalt no more be termed forsaken; neither shall thy land any more be termed desolate: but thou shalt be called Hephzibah, and thy land Beulah: for the Lord delighteth in thee, and thy land shall be married." In the margin on the side of the page it stated, "Hephzibah, that is, my delight is in her, Beulah, this is, married.

I began to rejoice in the Lord. I went to my favorite prayer spot and began to worship God. Through the scripture God let me know that my name would be changed. The reproach of divorce, the desolation of my circumstances was going to change. I would be married. I didn't understand how or when. I didn't know if God would reconcile my husband and I. However, I did not believe God intended reconciliation. Somehow in God's predestinated plan and I would remarry. At that moment I didn't try to figure it out. God said it. I received it.

Another Saturday evening, I prayed for God to save my unsaved male friend and to intercede in his life. God simply said, "Yes." I interpreted it to mean that God would save him. However, I now realize God may only have been saying that He would intercede in his life. The very next day, God began to deliver my friend. He was bound by depression. He associated with family and friend that brought him down. His home was painted in all dark colors. As I drove up to his house, his sibling was moving out of the house. Also, one of his tenants was moving. I could not believe God had moved in less then twenty four hours. When I went into the house, I was even more surprised. The living room was painted white, and my friend was planning on painting every room a lighter color. Tropical plants were now in the living room. His spirit of depression was lifting. I told God, He was just awesome! Because of these immediate answers to prayer, I questioned whether God had chosen my friend to be my husband. After a period of time, I began to believe he was God's choice for my future. As long as he was God's choice, I could wait for him to surrender his life to God.

As he began to come to church, I was faced with another problem. If he was God's choice for my life and he became saved, how could I marry him? Although I accepted salvation at a church that believed in divorce and remarriage under certain circumstances, I was now a leader in another church that did not believe in remarriage. God's promise became a source of joy and pain. For over two years, I wrestled with the consequences I would face if I remarried. I decided that there were three criteria that had to be met in order for me to remarry. 1) The man had to be saved and love God. 2) The man had to love me and put me on a pedestal; and, 3) It had to be all right with my church. Although the first two criteria were achievable, I saw no way in which the third criteria could be met. I wanted my pastor to perform the wedding. My pastor was my spiritual father, and I wanted Daddy to be proud and rejoice as I went down the wedding aisle. I did not want him to have to silence me (Silencing is an ostracizing discipline in the church where the individual can not function in any auxiliaries or testify. In some churches the person silenced was/is required to sit in the back of the church.)

Many times during the first year of this struggle, I sat in service and thought of what would happen if I remarried. I looked at my minister friends when they say in the pulpit. They were like brothers to me. I thought of how their attitudes would change towards me if my male friend became saved and we married. I would be considered a backslider living in sin. And because of this sin, they would feel I was going to hell. I pondered how I could remain in my church and still feel free to worship God when my brothers and sisters considered me as living in sin. Tears came to my eyes on many occasions. I asked God, "How can these things be?" I began to study the scriptures regarding divorce. My personal attitude was changing. I did not clearly see the interpretation of the scriptures that our church organization believed.

As I attended other churches with my pastor when he had preaching engagements, I began to consider whether that church could be a church I would attend when I remarried. I did not want to leave my church, but I didn't think I could survive the fall from grace or the ending of my church activities if I were silenced. I could not bring reproach upon my church by openly disobeying the doctrine. I considered that it might be better for me to leave the church when I remarried. However, no church we visited agreed with my spirit. I became sad every time I considered leaving my church home. But I knew God's promise, and it conflicted with my church doctrine.

My first external conflict between my changing views and that of our church teaching was in a class I taught for our bible school. One of the lessons particularly addressed divorce and remarriage. I explained to my students that the personal opinion of the teacher should not be given in the class. Just as our pastor had the responsibility of teaching the doctrines of the organization, I had the responsibility of presenting the same teachings as our pastor. I explained the doctrine of our organization and compared it to the teachings of our pastor. Although the organization did not allow for divorce, our pastor believed in divorce under certain circumstances. However, I concluded the lesson by advising that each person must go to God for his/her own answers. I had to be true to what I believed, but I did not want to appear to be in conflict with my pastor.

The conflict between God's promise and our church doctrine increased. During two different revivals, I sought God with the intension of giving up my relationship with my male friend. In both instances, God did not answer me directly. On the first occasion, I had determined that I would completely surrender to God's will with regard to my relationship with my friend. (I used the term friend because we never fully considered ourselves boyfriend and girlfriend or dating.) I told God, "Whatever you say, I will obey. If it is to end the relationship, I will do it immediately." I stood on the prayer line anxiously awaiting God's word. As I stood before the evangelist, I stood with baited breath waiting for a Word of Knowledge from the Lord. Then God really messed me up. He did not even hint at what I should do. He didn't even address my issue. Instead, the man of God told me that I had been sitting on prophecy for the past three years. This was an accurate Word from God;; and I received it but I laughed within myself. It was as if God was the parent who ignores His child's question because the parent had answered that question several times before.

Do you know there is a time when God will ignore your questions? Could it be that God was more interested in what I did with my spiritual life and the ministry He had placed within me? His focus was not my focus at that moment. It was true. I had been prophesied to and received a Word of knowledge regarding the ministry of prophecy in my life. (Notice, I use the term the "ministry of prophecy" rather than the gift of prophecy.) I walked away from that line no longer focusing on whether to end the relationship, but questioning how I was sitting on prophecy. What was prophecy? I was not a prophet, but prophecy was within me. God was more concerned with my spiritual walk than my natural walk. After researching the various definitions of prophecy, I understood that God was telling me I was sitting on my call to ministry. I was sitting on my calling to exhort and encourage through the Word of God. I stopped asking God about my relationship and lived my life from day to day building up spiritual inner man.

One Saturday, my pastor informed me that I was being appointed as the Sunday School Superintendent. I currently was the Assistant Superintendent. I became stressed and sought God once again regarding my relationship with my male friend. How could I accept this important leadership position knowing that when God saved my friend; and if we married, I would be "silenced". I looked forward to the challenge of being the Sunday School Superintendent but how could God fulfill His promise? How could I find happiness in marriage when immediately after I said, "I do," I would have to give up this leadership position?

We were in revival. (Surprisingly with the same evangelist that I mentioned above.) At the end of his sermon, he stated that everyone had made at least one decision they regret. He invited everyone to come to the altar with that one decision. I was having a pity party and felt that my one decision was when I first married my ex-husband. My life would have been different, and I would not have been faced with the question of remarriage. I came to the altar telling God that I was willing to give up this man for the sake of doing His work. He was more important than any man. The altar was full. Like everyone else, I had tears running down my face as I knelt before God. When the man of God prayed for me, he said, "Be still and continue to work." Shortly after that, my pastor's wife, Dr. Phyllis Carter, laid her hand on my back. She said, "You already have the victory." Although I did not feel victorious, I received the statement from both the evangelist and my pastor's wife into my spirit.

It was two years later that I fully understood the importance of my pastor's wife's statement. God was preparing to bring about a radical change in my church regarding the teachings on divorce and remarriage. Although I knew God was capable of sending me a man who loved Him and who would love me, I did not consider or have faith to believe that God would move in the area of my third criteria. I can only say that when God makes a promise to you, take the limits off of God. You have to think outside the box of your present truth and explore the fact that He is able to do exceedingly, abundantly above what you can think or ask.

In my church, change was subtle and miraculous. My pastor's wife was the founder of a women's ministry entitled Women's Christian World (WCW). The annual retreat was held in January. Although I was unable to attend that year, a friend loaned me a copy of one of the seminars. I listened to the cassette while I was at work. Two seminars were conducted by a Baptist pastor who was a dean in a college in Virginia. He boasted of having a Pentecostal flair. In one of the seminars he told the story of one of his church member who remarried. This young woman married a man who immediately began to commit adultery. He eventually left her and later divorced her. The young lady was faithful to God and her church. She caught the attention of one of the deacons. They fell in love and planned to marry. She came to this pastor broken, feeling guilty, and crying because she had been taught that if she married this man, she would cause him to commit adultery. Although she was legally divorced, she was still married in the sight of the church.

The pastor counseled her by first addressing her marital statue. Although she was divorced according to the law, she was using a church definition of marriage. Therefore, if she used a church definition of marriage, she must use a church definition of a husband. The pastor began to examine each scripture that gave the qualifications and characteristics of a husband. After reading each scripture, the pastor asked the young woman if her husband met this biblical definition. For each scripture, her husband did not meet the definition. The pastor concluded that since her husband had not met the biblical standards of a husband, she really did not have a husband. If she did not have a husband from a biblical standard, she was not bound by a biblical standard of marriage that kept her bound to this man when she was legally divorced. The couple married. God put His stamp of approval by immediately giving them promotions on their jobs and improving their living situation.

The pastor concluded this topic by sharing another story he shared at a Baptist deacon's convention. He stated that a man can choose to live his life recklessly. He can become a criminal, sell and buy drugs, sleep with several women and have children by each of them. He then is arrested for murder and accepts Jesus as his savior while he is in jail. When he is released, the church will do all it can to encourage him to grow in God and to become all that he can be. His past transgressions are forgiven and forgotten. Another young man who is raised in the church, lives his life according to God's principles. He goes to school and gets a good job. He is faithful to one woman and gets married. Unfortunately the marriage doesn't work out, and he finds himself divorced. In the Baptist church, a deacon is not allowed to be divorced. Therefore this young man is not allowed to grow. He is criticized, scorned and cannot hold positions in the church he loves so much. The pastor concluded his presentation of the deacon's convention by saying, "So men, if you want to get rid of your wives; kill them, because the church will accept a murdered before it accepts a divorced man."

When I heard this I hollered. The statements made in the seminar were not biblical, but they made common sense. The simplicity of their message set me free. According to man's law, I was legally free to remarry. My husband had not fulfilled the biblical definition of a husband. God had not joined us together. Therefore, from a common sense point of view I was not bound to him. Just as important for those who may have considered me to be in sin if I remarried, the grace of God would be sufficient. If the Apostle Paul, who was a murderer, could become an anointed vessel used by God, then certainly a woman who remarried could also be a chosen vessel o God.

I don't know how logical this trend of thought may seem to some, but at that moment, two plus two equaled liberty. At that moment, weights dropped from my shoulders and I hurried into my co-workers office. I needed to borrow her office a moment so that I could shout and praise God. How simple it all seemed. Although I had been married for over ten years, I had never had a husband who met the biblical definition of a husband. I did not have a protector/provider. My husband had not loved me as Christ loved the church. At the moment, it no longer mattered what anyone else thought of my marital status.

That was a personal victory and a personal change, but God was moving on a larger scale. One Sunday, my pastor stood in the pulpit and stated that we needed to rethink the issue of divorce and remarriage. I could not believe my ears. I could have fainted and fallen off of the pew. He continued to state that there were circumstances and situations where the couple married but had not been joined together by God. He asked the question, what happens when the woman has been deceived? He shared with us the true story of a couple that married when my pastor was a young man. The husband had been saved but was not delivered from homosexuality. To all appearances he was heterosexual. When the couple married, the young man was not able to consummate the marriage, even after several attempts. Although the marriage was not consummated, the young woman was advised that she could not annul the marriage. If she did separate or divorce her husband, she could not remarry. Although this young woman of God had been deceived, she was now forced to face her entire future alone. My pastor asked us to consider the couple whose parents forced them to marry because the girl became pregnant. Surely God had not joined these couples together. It was time for our church to re-evaluate our views on divorce and remarriage. In amazement, I questioned God, "Can this be real? Are you really making a change? God what are you doing?"

This was the beginning of a difficult period of doctrinal change for my church. There were seminars and pastoral teachings to address the new understanding of the scripture and life circumstances that my pastor had. During this period of time, my pastor also began to address the controversial subject of women in ministry. He had always believed women could preach and allowed them to do so in our church. However, women did not hold the title of minister, nor were they licensed. The issue of women in the pulpit overshadowed the doctrine changes regarding divorce and remarriage.

There were many who did not agree with the changing tide of the church. Some members left the church believing in their hearts that our pastor was leading the church into sin. But for people like me, it was a breath of life breathed into a dying area of my life. What I thought could never be possible was slowly becoming a reality in my church. My third criteria to remarry, was now possible. Oh the joy that filled my heart on the day my pastor told me that when I remarried, he would perform the wedding. The promise God made to me several years earlier seemed more obtainable. When my pastor's wife told me I "already had the victory", God was letting me know He had a plan and He was in control.

PRAYER

Father God, in the name of Jesus Christ, thank you for your promises and for the assurance that your word will go out and not come back void. Thank you for moving and interceding in our lives. Help us to hold on to your promises. Thank you for giving us strength to hold on to your work until it is fulfilled. Lord, don't let us waiver by what we see, think or feel. Help us to remember that you are in control, and there is nothing impossible or too hard for you to do! Amen!!!

Chapter 9

FACE TO FACE
(Facing the Inner Me)

The person who has been hurt or rejected as a result of a failed relationship may be adamant about not remarrying or seeking a relationship with another person. The pain of a broken heart can be so intense that we feel like we want to die. The emptiness and rejection that we feel is not an experience that one willingly wants to experience again. Therefore, the person may withdraw from relationships altogether. Many homosexuals and lesbians have stated that the reason they prefer a person of the same sex is because they experienced a hurtful, failed relationship with a person of the opposite sex. They have withdrawn from God's ordained male/ female relationship because they do not want to be hurt or made vulnerable again. However, they can still experience a broken heart. Heartbreak is not something we can run away from.

Every individual fancies himself or herself in love with someone who in reality doesn't love them, or who may not even know they exist. As teenagers, we called it "crushes;" possibly because one felt like their heart was crushing every time they saw the person they were in love with. We must treat our relationships like riding a bike, or a horse. If we fall down, we must get back up. We cannot allow the fear to trust or love again to become a stronghold within our lives. It will paralyze our lives, and our future. The way to overcome this fear is to immediately return to the thing that threw you and confront it. You get back on the bike; you get back on the horse and you get back behind the driver's seat. You confront your fear face-to-face.

I was a new driver when I had my first car accident. I was alone in the car with my infant son. It was raining, and I was driving down Hempstead Avenue. in Jamaica, New York. A car cut across me from a side street. There was insufficient time to stop. I saw the crash coming, but there was nothing I could do. My Cadillac (the tank), hit the car on the driver's side. I sat stunned. The driver of the other car looked at me, and I saw the demons staring at me. He sped off without a second glance. Although neither my car nor I and my son were hurt, I sat in my car in the left lane afraid to move the car.

Eventually, I pulled the car over to a pay telephone. I had no intension of continuing driving home. However, after several phone calls, I was unable to reach help. I reluctantly accepted the fact that I would have to drive home. I had no choice but to face my fear and drive. I was shaking and crying, but I drove. I told myself, "You can not fall apart and make it home at the same time." I could not be distracted by what had happened to me, so I drove. At every light I allowed myself the release of tears. But when the light turned green, I had to go on. Eventually, I arrived at my destination. As traumatic as that experience was, it is now a memory.

Just because you have been sideswiped in life by a broken heart, you can't stay stuck in the middle of the road. You have to continue to move forward. Shed the tears that you must, but keep yourself together enough to face your future. God has given you a green light to reach the "expected end" that He has for you.

We must put having a broken heart into perspective. Having a broken heart is like the pain of giving birth. It should be a pain that we eventually forget. When I was pregnant with my first child, my mother told me about the pains of labor and the actual delivery. I was happy with my pregnancy until that moment. I do not like pain. I avoid it at all costs. Then my mother dropped that bomb. "THE DOCTOR WILL CUT YOU." If it were at all possible, I would have stopped being pregnant at that moment. "What do you mean the doctor is going to cut me? Wait a minute, you mean I have to experience pain?" I was not ready to hear this. However my mother told me one other important thing. "It is a pain you will forget." How could she tell me that I could experience hours of pain, a doctor would cut me and I would forget the pain of that experience? She explained that it was a pain that a woman has to forget; otherwise a lot of us would not have been born. Although ever birth experience is different, most women will testify of their pain. Yet they have more children. Who would volunteer or willingly experience the pain my mother described more than once? Women remember the experience, but they don't continue to feel the pain. It is only as they begin to prepare for the birth of the next child that women say, "Now I remember this feeling!"

In the same way, everyone experiences a broken heart at least once in their lifetime. It may vary in intensity, but it is inevitable. We cannot run away from pain. A broken heart is a pain that should eventually go away. We will remember the experience that caused the pain, but we don't have to hold on to the pain. We don't have to be afraid of letting ourselves love again. When we experience a broken heart, we should give ourselves, and our pain over to God. He will help us to have peace. He will ease the pain. St. John 14:27 states that the Holy Ghost is a comforter, and that God will give us peace. "Peace I leave with you, my peace I give unto you: not as the world giveth, give I unto you. Let not your heart be troubled, neither let it be afraid." St. Matthew 11:28 states; "Come unto me, all ye that labour and are heavy laden, and I will give you rest." When we experience a broken heart, we can rest in God by allowing the Holy Ghost to be a comforter.

I remember being in a revival service near the time of my wedding anniversary. I was thinking about the loss of my husband, when I heard the voice of God saying to me, "I know how to be a husband. I'm your husband." The spirit of peace fell on me, and I literally felt the arms of God embrace me. The Holy Ghost is a comforter. God's word is true; it does not come back to Him void.

We cannot be afraid to open our hearts. We cannot afford to withdraw into a shell because of a broken heart. We have got to take a chance of being hurt again, of being vulnerable in order to be whole. Yet this is also easier to say than to do. I did not realize I wasn't ready to remarry and live happily ever after. I was praying for God to move, to send me my "Mr. Right". Yet when I thought I was about to remarry, I found myself in a state of panic.

I was holding on to God's promise to me that I would be married. I had a relationship with a friend whom I thought might be my future husband. He wasn't saved, but I knew that if he were God's choice, God would take care of his salvation. The church was in revival, and I attended the noonday service. The evangelist called me and two other sisters out to minister to us. He stated that our testimonies were going to change from "God is able," to "look what the Lord has done." When the evangelist ministered directly to me, he told me that I wanted to speak to my pastor about my situation. I should get ready to speak to him. Oh I rejoiced in the Lord. God was going to do this! I was so excited. God was a wonder; He was awesome!

Well, that was Friday afternoon. On Monday, while driving with my pastor, he began an unusual conversation regarding my ex-husband. I asked my pastor why he asked me the questions he asked. He responded that although I was saved, everyone wants companionship. I said within myself, "God! What are you doing? Is this what the evangelist was talking about? Am I supposed to talk to my pastor now?" I found myself sharing information about my relationship with my friend with my pastor. Imagine my surprise when my pastor stated that he already knew about the young man. I became more excited, "Look at me God!" The evangelist had spoken on Friday, and God moved on Monday. Hallelujah!!! I rejoiced in God for two days before it really hit me. This could really be going down. God could continue to move, and I would be remarried. I literally broke out into a cold sweat. I panicked. I realized that I wasn't ready. Fear took control. All of the "what ifs" entered my mind. The fear of making the wrong choice and fear of being hurt or abandoned again ruled the moment. I withdrew. I avoided my friend for a week. God said, "I have more work to do in you. You still feel vulnerable. You are afraid your Dr. Jeckle will turn into Mr. Hyde."

God revealed to me not only my fear but, also that I was questioning my judgment. After all, my first "Mr. Right" turned out to be "Mr. Wrong". How did I know I wasn't being led by self rather than by God? My confidence in my judgment was broken. My self-esteem was like shredded wheat. No, I was not ready. God let me know that fear, and all those other emotions, had to be overcome before He could bless me with the man of His choice. Questioning my judgment, and the lack of confidence in my decision making, hindered me from hearing God's voice. How could I be sure whether God, or my flesh was speaking? In other words, I was not trusting God. I should have known His voice in this area of my life. But instead, I needed a spiritual hearing aide. I needed to trust God more and build my faith in Him for this area of my life. I had to be able to separate my emotions from God's spirit.

I determined that I could not make a move unless I knew it was God's will. I had to trust Him to not lead me in the wrong path or to choose the wrong mate. Proverbs 3:5 states that we must trust in the Lord with all of our heart and not to rely on our ability to understand. We should acknowledge Him in all our ways, and He will guide us. He will lead us and guide us if we trust Him. Even if we are not confident in ourselves, we have to be confident in Him. He will not lead us astray.

When it comes to relationships, we have to be led by the spirit and not by our carnal mind. If, we are led by the Spirit, we will have confidence in God's ability to lead us down the path, that will lead to our happiness. He will not allow us to settle for the person that does not meet His will. If we allow ourselves to be led by the spirit, we don't have to lean on our abilities or be fearful that we will end up with the wrong mate. It is only when we focus on our flesh that we must question our judgment. We might want him tall, dark and handsome. We make our choice by our senses; by what we see, hear and feel. When "Mr. Tall, dark and handsome" comes along, we say, "This must be God. After all, God does know my taste." We do not take time to consult God. Then we wonder why this man turned out to be a scrub. God was not sending tall, dark and handsome. He was sending, tall, fair, and OK to look at. When God's choice came along, we sent him away because he wasn't the choice of our senses.

Because I was tired of being alone, I allowed my carnal

mind to cloud my spiritual mind. I had a promise from God to remarry. I had a prophecy, but the man that I was talking to was not God's choice. God had a purpose for the relationship, but he was not Gods' choice for my future. Because I questioned my judgment and lacked confidence in my decisions, I held on to the relationship for several years. I could hear God's voice saying this man was not the one for me. But I also questioned whether this was my fear and doubt rejecting God's choice. Because I didn't let go of this relationship, I may have missed the one who was God's choice. Until I can allow the spiritual mind to take control, and I can overcome my insecurities, I will not be ready to remarry. It has been eleven years since God's first promise. It had been nine years since God renewed the promise when I had the conversation with my pastor. Yet I still have not overcome this area in my life. I am learning to know His voice within me when it comes to relationships. But I haven't arrived yet. I still feel anxious as month after month passes and I have not met God's choice for my life. I found myself making plans for how to meet someone or to call on an old male friend. Yet each time, I heard God's voice saying, "Didn't I tell you to let me do it?" I smiled to myself and said, "Ok Lord, not my will but your will be done."

No matter how I feel, or the pressures from the enemy, I still know it has to be God's choice and God's time. So many children of God have made the wrong choice because they convinced themselves they were hearing God's voice when it was their flesh speaking. Although all the signs were there, although people, even their pastors warned them, they are convinced that God gave them this person. What we have to understand is that even if the person is God's choice, we have to wait on God's timing. God may be working something out of the person. God may be customizing the mate that's His choice. We move ahead of God, and then get angry with God asking Him why He allowed us to get into this mess. God responds that He spoke, but we wouldn't listen. We were looking for the neon "stop" sign or a talking donkey.

Although it is hard to hear from God when we allow our emotions to rule, it is even harder to hear from God when the enemy has us questioning our judgment or strips us of our confidence. The relationship I had been in had the purpose of restoring some of my confidence in myself as a woman. It combated the spirit of rejection and the thought that I was not desirable. It combated Satan's constant voice whispering that no man would want me. As our relationship began to grow to become more than friends, I began to think that he was God's choice for my future. Although he was not saved, I told him that if he were God's choice, then I would wait for him to surrender his life to Christ. When the evangelist prophesied to me, God exposed dark areas in my life. He helped me to understand that I had a stronghold to overcome before God could fulfill the prophecy. My error was in allowing my carnal mind to confuse my spiritual mind. When I learned what God wanted me to know; when I overcame my panic and began to trust that God would not allow me to make a wrong choice, I did not want to let go of the relationship. It served its purpose, and it was time for me to move on. However, I still said that if he were God's choice, I would wait. I didn't listen to the voice that occasionally said, "He is not the one." Although we loved each other, our life choices were different. Love would not make him choose to be saved. I had God's promise, the man of God's prophecy, and a man that I loved. Part of me felt like I couldn't get anyone else. The low self-esteem I had kept me from venturing out to other possibilities. When someone else did come into my life, I couldn't accept him because I was holding on to the relationship I had become secure in. I was in a comfort zone.

To this day, I still question whether I let God's choice go because I was afraid of a new relationship. I met a man who, within the course of an hour's conversation was swept off his feet. All we discussed was God and the church. I could not believe that he could become so interested in me after only an hour. Anything I wanted, I could have had. Yet I was afraid. I called it a fatal attraction. For two years, all I had to do was say the word. At the time, I did not conceive that God could move that fast. I was clouded by doubt. Now, I realize that God cannot only move that fast, He can sweep me off of my feet. There isn't anything too hard for God. What God has for me, and whom He has for me is pre-ordained. When I least expect it, God can make his move. While I'm looking to the right, God can come from the left. However, God has to work on me to deliver me from the fear of making the wrong choice; from questioning my judgment and from low self-esteem. When God sends a man into my life, I cannot be afraid. I have to know His voice and be able to receive Gods blessings. I don't want to reject my blessing by throwing up a barrier, or by constantly asking God, "Is this you?"

In order to be delivered, I had to identify the spirits that had me bound, turn myself over to God and take authority over these spirits. Although God exposed these strongholds, I allowed them to exist and continue to bind me. It is only as I am writing this segment that I am really realizing that I had the authority and power to be delivered even before God revealed these strongholds. The scripture states; "But ye shall receive power, after that the Holy Ghost is come upon you…" (Acts 1:8); "And these signs shall follow them that believe; in my name shall they cast out devils;" (Mark 16:17). Therefore I do not have to accept what Satan has placed into my mind. If I am trusting God, have kept my spirit man built up, and allow the Spirit of God to lead and guide me, I don't have to question my judgment.

I have walked with the Lord for eleven years since I first received God's promise to be married. Yet, I did not follow His word in the area of questioning my judgment or of having low self-esteem. In fact, I have been bound by low self-esteem for as long as I can remember. Romans 12:1-2 says that as a child of God, I needed to renew my mind. I knew the scriptures; I knew that I had power and authority but I did not apply it to this area of my life. I had been stuck. But even now, God is releasing me. The spirits of freedom and victory are flowing.

As I began to write this portion of the book dealing with the effects of divorce that cause one to question ones judgment, attack ones confidence and self-esteem, I felt the book taking a different turn. I was uncomfortable because I felt it moving to deal with two different messages. The book moved away from the problems that result from divorce, to the stronghold that the enemy had on my life in general. Although I connected the thoughts, they didn't flow as I put them on the paper. Little did I know that this was God beginning to release me, and healing was beginning to take place.

Yes, I stayed in a relationship too long questioning my judgment and my ability to hear the voice of God, but more was taking place in my mind as I wrote this segment.

When I wrote about the man who was immediately attached to me, I felt the spirit of depression take hold. A voice said, "He was the one for you. You let him go and now you'll never have anyone in your life. You blew it." It was the same spirit that made me question my worth that tried to convince me that I did not have what it takes to be attractive to men. I found myself trying to write through an increasing pain. But a ray of light began to appear as I began to think about the unlimited power of God.

The reality is that I know neither of the two men were God's choice for my future. But in looking back, I can see how my experience with them helped to rebuild my self-esteem and to show me the strongholds in my life. Although I often said God could change my circumstances at anytime, I now embrace the knowledge that when God moves, change will happen quickly. Like Job, my experiences have changed me to have a closer relationship with God. "I have heard of thee with the hearing of the ear, but now I seeth thee" (Job 42:5).

During the period of writing this segment of this book, I had a renewing of my mind. I had a release in my spirit, and I am writing with new freedom. I have talked about needing to be delivered and put the burden of being delivered on God. Yet God has been waiting for me to operate in the power and authority He has given me. All these years, I allowed these spirits to be a stronghold in my life when I had the power and authority to cast them out. I have taken authority over spirits in the deliverance of others, but did not think to look inward so that I could be delivered.

Over a year ago, God gave me a clue in a sermon He gave me, "The Enemy is the Inner Me!" I was later asked to do a seminar on that topic. God moved, and others were set free. I told myself I was somebody in God. The experiences of my youth and the results of my divorce attacked my self-esteem. I believed I was delivered through that sermon and seminar. I then experienced a series of events that pulled me back into the bondage of low self-esteem. Spirits can be cast out for a season, but they will return and try to get back in. The series of events opened the door for low self-esteem to re-enter. In addition, since I began writing this book, the attack on my self-esteem and confidence increased to a point greater than I have ever experienced. I found it attacking my thoughts, actions and even my physical mannerisms. I found myself playing solitaire on the computer with tears of depression rolling down my face. Even as one of my friends struggled with her own personal issues, I had to tell her that I could not afford to allow the attitude she was taking to take hold in my mind. If it did, it would cause me to completely give up. I may as well have rolled over and died. Like Jessie Jackson, I needed to 'keep hope alive' or shrivel up and die. I knew that I was under attack, I knew who the enemy was; and I knew he did not have the final victory, but he was winning the battle.

One weekend, I told myself, "you have to get angry at Satan. You have to fight back." I shut in and talked to God and Satan. I was determined to have victory. The stronghold of Satan was loosening. Then two days ago, I was reading the last pages of Rev. Tina Baker's book, "Feeling Trapped But There's a Way Out." and I saw myself. We had also had a conversation on how Satan made her feel ugly and not desirable. I saw myself again. She told me, "I know how you feel." In addition, someone we knew just had a storybook wedding. Although I rejoiced in her blessing, I know others who would become depressed because they asked God, "What about me?"

If these attractive women who have no trouble getting male attention could become depressed and deal with self –esteem issues, I struggled to keep my positive mindset of, "If God did it for her, then He is no respecter of persons and my turn is coming." But like Tina said, "There are times when I don't feel attractive, when I don't feel the hope of having someone in my future." But as I thought of Tina's book and read how God delivered her, I knew the same thing was happening for me. God was renewing my mind. As I set down and began to write, the words took a direction of their own. Suddenly, it hit me in the face. "Why have you allowed the enemy to bind you for all these years? You talk about the power, but you haven't used it in your own life to take authority over the spirit of low self-esteem. You say the words, "I am more than a conqueror, I am a royal priesthood, I am an anointed woman of God," but you allowed

Satan to sucker punch you.

I am who God says I am, and I can do all things through Christ who strengthens me. Therefore low self-esteem has to go. Even now, I take authority over that spirit and command it to depart never to return to this vessel. I am beautiful and desirable. In fact, I am a blessing waiting to be found. (He that findeth a wife, findeth a good thing.) God has ministered to me in this area many times but I am finally feeling freedom. I don't need a man to validate me. God has validated me! I don't need the approval of people, if God has approved me. Yes I understood that there is a lot of competition out there. My church is full of beautiful women of God who have it going on. But I have to know that I have it going on as well. The man(husband) God has for me is taylor-made. He will look upon me as his prize. He may see other jewels, but he will choose this diamond. Anyone else that may come into my life and pass through is only an imitation of the real thing that God has for me.

Why have I been bound, when God set me free? I did not have the mind of Christ in this area of my life. Jesus knew who He was. He walked in confidence and authority. He was not moved by the world standards. Neither did He allow Himself to be bound by others opinions. All of my life, I dealt with the opinion of others which attacked my self-esteem. But now I know, it is only God's opinion of me, and my opinion of myself that matters. If I walk uprightly before Him, no good thing will be withheld from me. Therefore, I have to question whether the relationship is a "good thing". I can now realize that God has something better in store for me. However, He could not bless me until I was ready. I had to overcome low self-esteem so that when God's choice comes, I will not think I am unworthy. I will not question whether this can be real, because I will expect nothing but the best from God. I deserve the best.

I know I have deviated from the flow and direction of this particular portion of the book. However, what you have just read is deliverance in action. I cannot explain the excitement and release I feel. Oh yes, the enemy is trying to tell me that he is not letting go that easily, but I have already won this battle. I am who God, and I, say I am. I was waiting for God to move; and like Dorothy from the Wizard of Oz; I had the power to be delivered all the time. I just didn't realize it.

If Satan has you bound, take a leaf from these pages. You are not weak; you are not a wimp. If you have the Holy Ghost, you have the power to treat on serpents. You have the authority over the demons that are plaguing your life. Lay hands on your self and command the demons to depart and go to the dry places. They will not leave willingly. They will even persist to see if you mean business. But continue to take authority until you are delivered. Every time doubt enters your mind, tell Satan, "No weapon formed against me shall proper," and take authority. The enemy is fighting me even now, but I am taking my own advice. I will be able to look low self-esteem in the face and say, "Is this the one that had me bound for so long?" I will know that this spirit; this stronghold, was broken as a result of writing this book and facing my fears.

Chapter 10

—•—

ICE ON THE FIRE

Several months after my husband left me, I received the monetary inheritance from my father's death. God released it just in time to prevent a utility shut-off; to pay rent arrears and to buy my children much needed clothing. I took care of all of my responsibilities but had done nothing for myself. Women's Christian World (WCW) was expanding to California. All of the women of my church were invited to go with my pastor's wife to the first meeting of the California branch of WCW For once in my life, I had an opportunity and money to travel. I made up my mind to treat myself to the trip. I was always doing for others, but this trip was for me. I was excited about the thought of traveling on a plane for the first time. I would be traveling with my pastor' wife and her armor bearer. God set it up so that only the three of us were going to California. For the first time, I didn't have to struggle to pay for something I wanted. There was a revival going on in my spirit. After being emotionally drained and beaten up for several months, I rejoiced in my upcoming vacation to California. I was on fire spiritually.

One evening, I received a telephone call from one of the sisters of the church. Although we were friendly, she was not someone who usually called me. Her conversation was friendly. She invited me to attend a Saturday morning breakfast fellowship. At first, I felt honored. However, she then began to talk about the scheduled trip to California. She told me she had previously attended a WCW meeting in the Bahamas and was disappointed because the retreat had not met her expectations. She hinted that I might be disappointed after making the financial sacrifice of traveling to California. She had scrimped and saved money to go to the Bahamas, but then regretted spending the money that she needed to pay her living expenses. She didn't know that I had sufficient funds to go to California fifteen times over. She implied that Dr. Carter was misdirecting me by encouraging me to spend money I could not afford. By this time, I knew something was radically wrong with this phone call. Although I didn't know what motivated this phone call, I knew it was not from God.

I questioned why this sister was trying to discourage me. I was on fire with expectation for this trip, and here she was putting ice on my fire. I was not going to be discouraged by her phone call. A fire had been lit in me, and I would not allow anyone to put it out. However, I still questioned God as to why she called. The spirit of God led me to discuss this conversation with a specific friend. Before I could get a few sentences out, my friend said, "I told her not to talk to you." This sister had spoken with my friend prior to calling me. In truth, she had done it out of concern. She didn't realize she was being used by the enemy. Apparently, she met my husband on the bus and he discussed his version of our separation. Whatever he said to her convinced her to reach out to me in concern. I won't say her motives were all pure. After all, she did undermine Dr. Carter. I don't think that she wanted to deliberately hurt me. However, she had been advised to leave the situation alone. I thank God that the Holy Ghost did not allow me to receive her words. God had a life-changing experience waiting for me in California.

When God gives you something, you cannot allow anyone to persuade you, discourage you or put out your fire. The thought of just going to California with Dr. Carter set a blaze in my spirit. I had been discouraged for so long, and the flames of encouragement were ignited. Yet the phone rang. Someone was standing there with a bucket of ice ready to extinguish the flames. They didn't just have a bucket of water. Although the water would have also put out the fire, it might have missed a spot and allowed the flames to rekindle.

But the ice would have melted on any spot where there was heat. As it melted, it would have ensured that all possibilities of the fire re-igniting was killed. Once the fire and heat are gone, any ice left not melted remains on top as a reminder that a flame was once there.

We must recognize the ice carriers. We can not allow them near our flames. Yes, we can be so on fire that the blaze is intense. Heat rises and singes everything near us, but do we want even one piece of ice to touch our flame? Do we want to waste the energy of our flame on drying up the ice? I recognized the ice bucket for what it was and kept it away from my flame.

I boarded the plane in New York anticipating a move of God in California. My blessing did not come from the topics of the seminars or from the sermons preached. It did not come from fellowshipping with new sisters in Christ. When God wants to fuel your flame; when He wants to bless you, He often operates in the unexpected. I knew I would be blessed by this trip; I was already blessed just by being there. But I expected my blessing to come from within the confines of the conference itself. Although the sessions were excellent; and they were a blessing, they were not life changing. My life changing experience came from a shopping trip.

Dr. Carter and Rev. Johnson invited me to go shopping with them to buy perfume. Are you kidding, to be able to go shopping with the big wigs! I was honored. We went to one store, and Dr. Carter bought a bottle of perfume. We went to another store and finally ended up at Norstroms. First of all, I had never been in an expensive store like Norstoms. I had not even heard of the store as they did not have a branch in New York at that time. I looked around as we walked through the aisles. I decided to buy myself a bottle of perfume. Dr. Carter and Rev. Johnson left the perfume department to go to the shoe department. I told them that I would meet them there. I was now on a mission for myself. I knew nothing about perfume. I had previously bought a few Avon perfumes, but I considered most of their perfumes too expensive for my pocketbook.

I passed an aisle, and a saleswoman asked me if I wanted to try the new perfume fragrance 'With Love'. I said okay. When she sprayed that perfume, something clicked in my spirit, my body and my mind. The smell was delicious. Right then, I decided that I wanted the perfume. I didn't care what size the bottle was or how much it cost. I made a decision to purchase this perfume for myself just because I wanted it, just because I deserved to do something wonderful for myself. I was always giving to my husband and children and putting myself on the back burner. But that moment was all about ME.

The bottle of perfume symbolized the fact that I believed I was worth it. I deserved to have the finer things of life. I realized that it was not a crime to put myself first once in a while. Within seconds of smelling the fragrance, I was at the counter purchasing a bottle. The perfume cost $60.00. I didn't blink twice. I didn't stutter. I pulled out my wallet and paid the bill. As I spoke to the saleswoman, I learned another marvelous secret. They gave out free fragrance samples! Not only did I have my $60.00 bottle of perfume, I also had a sample of another fragrance by the same maker and several other fragrances.

I had a new outlook on life, and a new image of myself. I changed from a person who didn't spend $10.00 on a bottle of perfume to someone who didn't care what the price was. (Now, if I like the fragrance, I owe it to myself to buy it.) I would not spend $60.00 on a dress, but I didn't blink when it came to purchasing perfume. Oh, I didn't just run amuck. I didn't fill my dresser with hundreds of bottles of perfume. God does expect us to use wisdom. I learned the best seasons to buy perfumes. I learned how to encourage the salesperson to give me samples. (New York was not like California. California loads you up with samples knowing you will return. In New York, you've got to sweet talk the salesperson into giving you samples.)

With my new attitude, I also learned that I didn't have to spend money to take a moment for myself. I developed what I call, "Me Moments." I don't always have money to buy perfume, but I can still make myself feel special. Whenever I decided it was time for a 'me moment', I go to the perfume department at the major stores in the shopping mall. I smelled the fragrances of the perfumes I liked. I talked to the saleswoman and I asked them to show me the latest perfumes. I first explained to the saleswoman that I am not purchasing at the moment, I am just looking and planning for when I have the funds to purchase the perfume. I discussed brands I like with them, and in return, they may tell me about a fragrance with a similar scent or one they like.

Some women can't handle window shopping; but my 'me moments' are not just a reward, they have a purpose. When I get my tax returns, or a large enough monetary gift, I go right back to the saleswoman who was pleasant to me. By the time I leave the department, we are both blessed. I have my perfume, and she has her commission.

All of this change came about because I decided to put myself first. From one bottle of perfume, I learned to take time for myself, to pamper myself, and to tell myself I am worth it.

Dr. Carter once made a statement that we should consider those who celebrate you. She asked the question, "Who celebrates you?" Those are the people you want around you. When she made that statement, I reflected on my life changing trip to California. Dr. Carter and Rev. Johnson celebrated me. People who celebrate you are people who fuel the flame within you; who celebrate the fact that you have caught on fire. I want to remind you to consider those people who you allow to get close to your flame. Are they bringing wood or combustible items to help you burn, or are they carrying a bucket of ice? I would have never had my life changing experience if I had listened to the sister who telephoned me that evening. Even with good intensions, a person carrying a bucket of ice has the potential to extinguish your flame. My brothers and my sisters, guard the flame that God has placed within you.

PRAYER

Father God in the matchless name of Jesus Christ give us eyes to see and ears to hear those who are fire extinguishers. Help us to know who celebrates us and who will fuel the flame you have sparked within us. Let us burn with anticipation for life changing experiences. Amen!!!

Chapter 11

YOU'RE NOT DAMAGED GOODS!!!

I have a friend who told me she did not want to get involved with a divorced man or a man with children, because she didn't want "Damaged Goods". That statement weighed heavily in my spirit. I then thought about the many times I saw television programs where a person was describing a possible blind date to a friend. The description was acceptable until the person was told he/she was divorced. Their friend immediately throws up their hands as if to say, "Stop right there." The red flag goes up, the huge stop sign springs into place, and the conversation comes to an abrupt halt. The friend is not interested in "damaged goods".

When I thought of this term, I thought to myself, "Is this how the world sees me? Is this how the church sees those of us who have been the survivors of a failed marriage?" We may already be experiencing feelings of rejection from our ex-spouses, but do we have to accept rejection from society and the church? Who determined that we were castaways; damaged goods, not to be considered for use? Who put the stamp "damaged" on our foreheads and placed us on the "damaged goods" shelf, or threw us in the trash can?" It doesn't matter whether you were the one who ended the relationship, or if you were the one abandoned. Others may still consider you damaged goods. The question is, "How do you view yourself?"

I refuse to be bound by the attitude that divorced people are damaged goods. After all that I have gone through, I refuse to allow someone else's attitude determine who and what I am. My marriage may have been damaged and discarded but I am not. I am what God says I am; a royal priesthood, the beloved of the Lord. So I ask the question, "Whose report will you believe?"

There was a time in my life when I thanked God for thrift shops, and garage sales. My finances were such that I could not afford to buy a lot of the things I needed from department stores. I knew all the thrift shops in several communities. Every Saturday I was at the thrift shop looking for something my family could use. I looked for yard sales and church bazaars. The marketing slogan for this type of shopping is, "One man's junk is another man's treasure."

Just because one person has determined that they have no use for an item, it doesn't mean the item has no value. In fact, there are people who specifically go to yard sales and bazaars looking for treasures sold at a ridiculously low price because the current owner doesn't know its value. Just because a person is no longer with their spouse, it doesn't mean that they have lost their value. Perhaps the spouse didn't realize the value of what he/she had. A knowledgeable person is able to identify a hidden treasure. Yes, it may be tarnished and in need of cleaning; a seam may have to be sown again, but it is still an item of value.

One Saturday, I rushed to a church bazaar with the expectation of running in for five minutes to find books to purchase. I was on a time schedule and needed to run back out quickly. They were having a $3.00 bag sale. A bag sale is when you squeeze as much clothing into a bag and pay one price for the entire bag. Because I was in a rush, I didn't want to spend the time necessary to fill up a bag. But the woman at the entrance convinced me to take a bag. I half-heartedly walked around looking at items. Several times this one assistant came up to me asking me if I needed help and bringing me items to look at. She kept telling me that they had coats. I began to get annoyed because she kept bothering me, and you usually cannot or would not put a coat in a bag for a bag sale. I walked away, but she came again with a midriff fur coat. She told me to put it into my bag. I told her it wouldn't fit, and we weren't allowed to put coats in the bag for a bag sale. She insisted that I could take the coat. She balled it up so that it would fit into the bag and put it in. I decided not to argue any more, after all she was there to assist people. I found a few more items and left.

The next week I went with my pastor to a speaking engagement in the Bronx. I brought the coat with me to his house to show off my fur coat. When he looked at the coat, he became excited with disbelief. He could not believe I had bought the coat in a $3.00 bag sale. He then told me the approximate value of the coat was $800.00. It was a mink coat. I really began to praise the awesomeness of God. I didn't know the value of the coat when it was forced upon me. I resisted the woman to the point of getting annoyed. Yet all the time, God and the woman were trying to bless me with something of value that I could not afford. Just because I didn't know the value of what I had, the value of the mink coat didn't change.

For whatever reason, the person who owned the coat had no more use for it. It is possible the owner bought another coat. Maybe the owner didn't fit the coat any longer. Or maybe the owner died. Whatever circumstances were that brought the coat to the church bazaar, it didn't matter. The coat still had value.

Some of us who have experienced separation or divorce have been tricked into believing that we have no value. We are defective and damaged goods because we are no longer of use to our spouses. We have walked around with our heads hung down. We have considered ourselves like the lepers of old, "unclean". When asked our marital status, we hesitate and catch our breath before saying almost apologetically, "I'm separated or divorced." I say unto you now, don't accept what Satan has put on you. You are not discarded junk! You are someone else's treasure. Maybe your spouse was like me. He/she didn't know your value and therefore did not treat you with the special care you deserved. You need to realize they were just ignorant of your worth. When I learned the value of the coat, I got a different attitude. I appreciated the coat as a blessing. Although the owner of the mink discarded it, the coat became my treasure and my blessing from God. God may have someone out there who will look at you as the valuable treasure that you are. They will glorify and praise God for having found you on the rack of discarded goods.

Some of you may be saying, "I AM DAMAGED GOODS.

The experience of my life, and marriage has left me broken and torn!" This may be true, but are you non-repairable? If, my mink coat had a tear in the seam or needed to be cleaned or if there was a hole near the bottom where a long coat could be made into a long waistcoat, I still had a treasure. The coat would just need to be repaired. A person who knows the value of an item doesn't mind taking the time or spending the expense to repair the damaged area.

The person that drops an expensive Ming vase doesn't discard it because the handle broke off. The person first determines whether it can be fixed. Once the handle is glued back on, the naked eye cannot tell the damage. Under close inspection, one may see a flaw, and the vase may lose some of its value. However, it is still a valuable Ming vase. If you have been damaged, you are still repairable. God has someone who can look past your damage, invest in your repair and consider himself/herself blessed for having you in his/her life.

King Solomon with all of his royal wives and concubines did not write the Song of Solomon to a queen or princess. His heart went out to a poor shepherd girl. When she looked at King Solomon, she could not believe he had chosen her out of all the beauties around him. She didn't bring him wealth or property. Yet Solomon considered her a treasure, his beloved.

If you have walked around with your head hung down due to the stigma of divorce; if you have considered yourself discarded junk, go to your mirror and tell yourself that you are God's treasure. You are a blessing that is yet to be discovered. If there are damaged areas in your life that you have identified, begin to repair them. You never know when God will send someone who recognizes your value; who will see you as God sees you. You are His chosen vessel, His beloved. Some treasure hunter is still looking for you. But are you ready to be found?

In an episode of a comedy sitcom, a woman was insecure and jealous of her boyfriend's ex-girlfriend who came to town for a visit. She was overly consumed with jealousy, envy and doubt until she was actually introduced to the ex-girlfriend. The boyfriend stood between the two women. He introduced the ex-girlfriend as the woman who turned down his proposal of marriage. The current girlfriend's attitude immediately changed. Joy filled her face, and she embraced the woman saying thank you. Her expression of gratitude stated, "I am thankful that I have him because you turned him down. Your junk is my treasure!"

PRAYER

Father God, in the name of Jesus Christ, thank you for allowing us to realize that we are precious in your sight. We are not discarded junk or damaged goods. We are the beloved of God. There are some of us who are broken and have not overcome the low-self esteem issues that result from being separated or divorced. Renew their minds so that they can realize their own value.

Chapter 12

LABOR PAINS

"Shall I bring to the birth, and not cause to bring forth? Saith the Lord: Shall I cause to bring forth and shut the womb? Saith the Lord" (Isaiah 66:9).

I have previously discussed God's promise for me to remarry. I must conclude this book by revisiting that promise. When it comes to the controversy of divorce and remarriage in my life, I have already received the victory. I was able to gain the victory by holding on to God's promise for my future. When God told me that I would remarry, He impregnated me with a promise. Yes, I would be married. I have held on to that promise and prophetic word for over ten years prior to the writing of this book, and for the year and eight months it has taken me to complete this book. God never told me how or when I would remarry. He didn't tell me what I would have to go through, or the tears and anguish I would experience reconciling God's promise with the physical reality of my circumstances.

As I previously shared, I came to understand that each individual must seek God for His will and direction for their own marital situation. God will back up whatever He tells you. If God says He will keep you, you'll be kept. If He tells you to go down the left road instead of the right, He knows the pitfalls or destruction awaiting you on the right road. If you seek God for His will in your marital situation, you can never go wrong.

When people have asked me if I would remarry, I have boldly told them, "yes." Not only would I remarry if I had the opportunity, but I also know that I will remarry. I have trusted God and taken Him at His word.

There are times when I've become discouraged. The waiting process is never easy. David said, "Wait, I say on the Lord" (Psalms 27:14). But, the waiting process is so important that he had to repeat it again. David admonishes us to wait and be of good courage. Don't grow faint or weary. " I had fainted unless I believed to see the goodness of the Lord in the land of the living" (Psalms 27:13).

We must remember that between the promise and the provision there is time. Everything that occurs during this time may not be pleasant. Yet, it can work together for our good. Joseph dreamed two dreams in which his family bowed down before him. They were prophetic dreams about his future leadership. It was his promise. Yet from the time of his dream, Joseph's brothers plotted to kill him. He was sold into slavery, falsely accused, thrown into jail, forgotten and overlooked by those who promised to speak on his behalf. He interpreted Pharaoh's dream and became a ruler of Egypt before his own dreams was fulfilled. Years passed between the promise and the provision. Joseph was able to look back at all he had gone through and acknowledge that it was God's will, and he fulfilled God's purpose. "And Joseph said unto his brothren, come near to me, I pray you. And they came near. And he said, I am Joseph your brother, whom ye sold into Egypt. Now therefore be not grieved, nor angry with yourselves that ye sold me hither: for God did send me before you to preserve life... And God sent me before you to preserve you a posterity in the earth, and to save your lives by a great deliverance. So now it was not you that sent me hither, but God: and he hath made me a father to Pharaoh, and lord of Egypt" (Gen. 45:4-8). David was anointed as the second king of Israel. Yet he killed a giant, won battles, fled for his life from King Saul and pretended to be insane before he was actually appointed king.

I've had to endure emotional changes, disappointments and heartaches since God gave me the promise. Although it has been years, God has not changed His promise to me. In the meantime, He expects me to trust Him to keep His word. The waiting process can just be a test. A preacher preached the message, "What Do You Do In The Meantime?" Do you give up on God? Do you pull back into old patterns and habits? When God hasn't answered quickly enough for you, do you go to "Plan B"?

During my waiting process, I have often taken matters into my own hands. I have made stupid mistakes because I became angry with God. I have shed unnecessary tears only to realize I had only myself to blame. I lost faith in the promise. I had to get to the point where I stopped focusing on when and how God was going to keep His promise and focus on serving God and fulfilling God's purpose for my life. The Word of God states that no man can serve two masters, and a double minded man is unstable in all his ways. Jesus admonishes us to seek first the kingdom of God and His righteousness, and God will take care of the things. While a spouse is not a thing, he/she is something that we can put before God. God cannot and will not bless us with a spouse when we put our desire for a spouse above our desire for Him.

I got to the place where I didn't care when or how God fulfilled His promise. I had to put God's promise on the back burner and turn up the heat in my relationship and service to Him. As my pastor once preached, I had to keep the "main thing" the "main thing". Because I trust the promise, I am living in expectation not desperation of the provision.

Although it has been years, God has always given me a jewel to hold on to. The first jewel was the prophetic word, "You already have the victory." The second jewel was the prophetic word to get ready to speak to my pastor. Several jewels were later given to me as specific prophecies of my remarriage. To be truthful, I did not accept the first of these latter prophecies. However, the second time someone spoke to me with almost the same information, I realized God was trying to give me something to hold on to. He was letting me know that although years had passed, God had not forgotten or cancelled His promise. Psalms 89:34 states, "My covenant will I not break nor alter the thing that is gone out of my lips." Time does not alter God's promise. Time is not an enemy. It is a tool God uses to prepare us for our destiny. We must remember that God has an "expected end" for our lives. Jeremiah 11:29 states, "For I know the thoughts that I think toward you, saith the Lord, thoughts of peace, and not of evil, to give you an expected end."

Several months ago as Bishop Carter was preaching, he quoted a scripture I had not heard before, Isaiah 66:9. "Shall I bring to the birth, and not cause to bring forth? Saith the Lord; shall I cause to bring forth and shut the womb? Saith the Lord." At that moment, the Lord spoke to me regarding His promise. He stirred the seed of the promise He had impregnated me with. He made my baby leap. Now that I have endured all these years nurturing the promise, God is preparing me for delivery. Now that I am experiencing labor pains, God will not allow me to have false labor. God has brought me to the birth. It is almost time to bring forth. I don't even have the man in my life yet, but it is time to bring forth. In Isaiah, God said that the restoration of Israel would be so quick and complete that it would be like a woman giving birth who goes into labor and immediately gives birth. It is so miraculous that she experiences no labor pains. God has not given me a time frame for the next step in fulfilling His promise. I only know that my time of delivery is near. God has not brought me this far and given me this assignment to expose my personal life just to allow His promise to be stillborn. He will not shut up the womb. He will not allow the promise to die within me. When I bring forth the promise, it will be so miraculous; it will be like the painless delivery mentioned in the book of Isaiah.

There is only one thing I knew for sure when I heard that scripture, this book or the completion of this book is tied into the fulfillment of God's promise. I started out writing this labor of love so that others who were experiencing the struggles I had faced could find a ray of hope. I am concluding this book with the knowledge that during the course of these past eighteen months, I moved to the final trimester of God's promise. I am at the point of delivery. When I bring forth the promise. When I walk down the wedding aisle, I will rejoice and God will be glorified. If anyone there is still struggling with the issue of my divorce and remarriage, I'll just laugh and say, "GET OVER IT!!!"

Beloved, what I am saying to you is that God has planted seeds of victory and destiny in you. He has an expected end for you.

However, to reach that end you must experience all of the aspects of your pregnancy. Every pregnancy brings moments of discomfort, joy and pain. My brothers and sisters, in order for you to bring forth, you had to go through the morning sickness of separation or divorce. You may have to change your diet in order to bring forth a healthy seed. You have been eating all of the lies Satan has been feeding you, and it has been making you mentally, emotionally and spiritually sick. You must feed on the Word of God. You will gain the spiritual strength needed to go through your labor and to bring forth.

Satan has tried to convince you that you have no future. But God is telling you that He is in control. He will not allow you to go through all of the processes of your pregnancy to abandon you or to abort what He has birthed in you. Your labor experience may cause you to bow over or to cry out in pain. But it is the proof that you are bringing forth. God said that He will not shut up your womb. You will survive your morning sickness of separation or divorce. You will overcome your emotional, spiritual and possibly physical changes. You may experience labor pains that make you wish you could start all over again. But after you give birth to your destiny; after you have experienced your victory; you will look at your baby and know that it was all worth it. You will see yourself as blessed. You will see yourself as the victor and not the victim. Like Joseph, you will acknowledge that God was in control. He had purpose. You survived labor pains and arrived at God's "expected end."

BE HEALED, BE WHOLE, BE FREE

"Trust in the Lord with all thine heart; and lean not unto thine own understanding. In all thine ways acknowledge Him, and He will direct thy paths" (Proverbs 3:5-6).

"Finally, brethren, whatsoever things are honest, whatsoever things are just, whatsoever things are pure, whatsoever things are lovely, whatsoever are of a good report; if there be any virtue, and if there be any praise, think on these things." (Philippians 4:8)

This book does not hold all of the answers, nor touch all of the possible issues of being a child of God who has experienced a failed marriage. It only touches the tip of the iceberg. The purpose of this book was to plant seeds of healing, to open up understanding and to give hope. King Solomon concludes the book of Ecclesiastes by stating, "Let us hear the conclusion of the whole matter". My brothers and my sisters let me give you this concluding message. "Get Over It." In other words trust in the Lord, and be healed, be whole, be free.

Printed in the United States
73660LV00005B/481-513

9 781420 874839